Sarah Flower is a working mother of two and knows how hard it is to balance work, family life and healthy eating. She uses her halogen cooker every day to produce healthy, flavourful recipes that are simple to follow and are loved by everyone, including her kids. She has written a number of books on cooking with a halogen oven including the bestselling *The Everyday Halogen Oven Cookbook*.

The Healthy
Halogen Cookbook

SARAH FLOWER

howtobooks

Constable & Robinson Ltd
55–56 Russell Square
London WC1B 4HP
www.constablerobinson.com

First published in the UK by How To Books,
an imprint of Constable & Robinson Ltd, 2013

A copy of the British Library Cataloguing in
Publication Data is available from the British Library

ISBN 978-1-9058-6296-2 (paperback)
ISBN 978-1-4721-1019-0 (ebook)

Printed and bound in the UK

1 3 5 7 9 10 8 6 4 2

Contents

Introduction

The halogen oven has proven to be a very popular gadget in the kitchen. The reasons people buy a halogen seem to vary: students buy it for convenience, caravanners love the fact it can be transported easily, the elderly like not having to bend to put something in the oven and families use it as an extra oven. Whatever the reason, this book will show you how to make the most of your halogen, and cook simple, nutritious meals for a healthier lifestyle.

The recipes in this book have been put together to provide you with a balanced diet, suitable for those following a low-salt or low-fat diet, or those watching their weight. They are also suitable for all the family as they are adaptations of everyday favourites.

One of the reasons we often struggle when trying to live a healthier lifestyle is because of lack of planning. This is especially true when it comes to food. Imagine coming home from work: you are hungry and want to eat something healthy, but what can you grab that is instant and satisfying? Often, this is the time when we go for the nearest chocolate bar, biscuits or packet of crisps. This is when planning ahead really works: if you know you have a busy day ahead, prepare something the night before that you can pop in the oven when you get home. Fill your freezer with homemade, healthy ready meals and for a guilt-free munch, bake some healthy cakes or biscuits, or simply pop some popcorn for a tasty, healthy snack in minutes.

The advantage of following a healthy diet is that it doesn't just benefit your health or waistline – it can also be kinder to your pocket. Even though your supermarket may have lots of 'bogof' deals and special offers, the majority of them will be for unhealthy, processed and snack foods. You may think you are getting a good deal but this is nutritionally empty food. On the other hand, eating wholegrain, fresh fruit and vegetables, good-quality meat and fish, along with pulses and beans, is not only good for your health but easier on your pocket.

As well as a whole load of wholesome recipes, this book contains information on how to use your halogen oven – I urge you to read this if you are new to this way of cooking as it will help when you want to create your own dishes. I have also included chapters on healthy eating and food swaps. The chapters are split into practical categories, including sections on salads and side dishes, which you may find useful as accompaniments to the main dishes.

I hope you enjoy the book and that it helps you lead a healthier lifestyle without feeling like you are depriving yourself!

Sarah x

How to use your halogen oven

Just as in my first halogen book, I want to show any newbie halogen users how to get the most from their machine.

Choosing the right machine for you

There are many types of halogen oven on the market, but they basically all work in the same way. The two main differences are the size of the bowl and whether the lid is hinged or not. My first machine was from JML, when halogens started to become popular. I wasn't entirely sure what to expect, and over time, it has been used more and more in our kitchen. Speaking from experience, I would opt for the largest bowl as this increases usability. You can also purchase an extender ring – a stainless-steel ring approximately 80mm high that sits on the rim of the bowl to provide extra cooking space. Since using the JML, I have progressed to the Flavorwave Turbo Platinum Oven. Out of all the machines I have used, this is one of the best: it has a hinged lid, digital settings, a three-speed fan and a preheat setting. I find unhinged lids can be a bit of a bugbear – I had a lid stand for my JML machine, though annoyingly this is an optional extra and is quite flimsy. If you can afford to buy a halogen cooker with a hinged lid, it is definitely a safer option.

How does it work?

A halogen oven consists of a large heat-resistant glass bowl with an electric halogen lid. The lid is heavy as it contains the heating element, fan, timer and temperature settings. The halogen bulb heats up the bowl and the fan moves the air around the bowl to create an even temperature. As it is smaller than a conventional oven, it heats up faster, reducing the need for long preheating and in some cases, reducing the overall cooking time. This makes it a very popular choice for those on a budget, living on their own or, like me, with a busy family. It also serves as a second oven and becomes invaluable at busy times like Christmas.

For safety reasons, the lid is fitted with a handle that has to be locked down for the machine to switch on. This means that when you lift the handle, the power automatically cuts off. If you have a machine with a hinged lid, you have to press the start button and remember to turn the machine off before lifting the lid.

The halogen oven does cook slightly differently to a conventional oven, so it is often a matter of trial and error when first starting out. I find cooking at a slightly lower temperature or cooking for less time usually gives the same results, so if you have a favourite dish you cook in a conventional oven, try it in the halogen bearing this in mind.

A halogen oven is not a microwave, so if you think you can cook food in minutes, you're wrong! It does, however, have a multitude of functions: defrosting, baking, grilling, roasting and steaming are all within its capabilities. Remember that to get the optimum benefit, air needs to circulate around the bowl, so ideally place the food on a rack and avoid the temptation to overfill the oven.

Getting the right equipment

This may sound obvious, but make sure you have a selection of oven trays, baking sheets and casserole dishes that fit in your halogen oven. You can use any type of ovenproof dish or tray: metal, silicon and Pyrex are all suitable. As halogen ovens are round it makes sense to use trays and stands of the same shape but just a little smaller so that you can remove them without burning yourself. When I first started using a halogen oven, it was frustrating to find that 80 per cent of my bakeware didn't fit in the machine. If money is tight, you can often find great casserole dishes at boot sales or charity shops, so don't think you have to spend a fortune on new cookware.

You can buy an accessories pack that contains a steamer pan, grilling pan, toasting rack and even an extension ring. These are highly recommended if you use your oven regularly. Many places on the web sell these, so a general search will point you in the right direction. Amazon is also a great place to look.

Let there be light

As experienced halogen-oven users will know, the halogen light turns on and off during cooking. This is not due to a faulty thermostat, as some may initially think. The light turns off when the programmed temperature is reached, then on again when it drops. Set the temperature and marvel at how quickly the oven reaches the required temperature – literally within minutes! I love the light: there is something quite cosy about walking into your kitchen on a winter or autumn evening to see the glow of the halogen cooker!

Size

The oven is small enough to sit on a worktop, but do bear in mind you'll need space to remove the lid, if it isn't hinged. The lid can get very hot and is large and heavy, so it is often a good idea to buy a lid stand, though be careful when using this as it takes some getting used to. Alternatively, you could place the lid on a heatproof surface, but be careful not to burn yourself or your worktop. As with all electrical appliances, do not let your children near it as the glass bowl gets very hot.

Timer

Halogen ovens come with a 60-minute timer and a temperature setting dial.

The Flavorwave Turbo comes with a digital timer and three fan settings. All halogens turn off when the timer setting has been reached. This means you can rest assured that if the phone rings or you are called away from the kitchen, your food won't spoil.

Carefully does it
Your oven should come with tongs to help you lift out the racks. They are quite useful, but I tend to use a more substantial pair of tongs. I find using oven gloves a necessity as they offer greater protection.

Foil and coverings
Foil is useful if you want to prevent food from browning too quickly. If you are using foil during the cooking process, you need to make sure it is secured tightly around the dish. The fan is very powerful, so if the foil is loose, it can float around the oven and could damage the heating element. Instead of using foil, try turning down the temperature, or place the food on the low rack, further away from the element, or use an extension ring.

High and low racks
Halogen ovens come with two standard racks: a low rack and a high rack. (It's worth buying an accessories pack which contains other racks if you think you're going to use your halogen a lot.) The racks can be used together so you can cook on two levels at once. The high rack is closer to the element, so use this when browning food. The low rack is used for longer cooking times. You can also cook directly on the bottom of the bowl; it works well but food will take a little longer to cook than on a rack as the hot air is not able to circulate as freely around the food.

Grilling
If you are grilling, you need to place the food on the highest possible rack. The high rack that comes with the halogen oven may not be suitable for 'quick' grilling, but if this is all you have it will work just fine but will take a little longer. It's worth purchasing an accessories pack, which contains a toasting rack (with egg holes). This can also be used as a grill rack. As this rack is closer to the element, grilling times are much faster – you can grill cheese on toast in 3–4 minutes.

Baking
Some people worry about baking cakes in a halogen oven. Make sure you set the oven to a low temperature for best results. If the temperature is too high and if you cook the cake for too long, you'll end up with a crusty brown top and soggy middle. Read more about baking on pp154-56 before trying some of the cake recipes and you'll see how simple halogen baking really is.

Preheat or no preheat?

Most recipes I have found on forums don't mention preheating. This is probably due to the speed the oven reaches its temperature; however, it is often worth turning the oven on 5 minutes before use, just to bring it up to the right temperature, especially when baking. I also found this to be the case when attempting to cook soft-boiled eggs. According to the Flavorwave recipe book, you should be able to cook a soft egg in 6 minutes just by placing it on the high rack. It didn't work, so I tried again in a preheated oven and the result was much more successful. Some machines have a preheat function, which preheats the oven to 260°C for 6 minutes, but others require you to set to the required temperature and turn on.

Finally... cleaning your oven

All halogen ovens are self-cleaning: add a cupful of water, a squirt of washing-up liquid and turn on the wash setting. The combination of the fan and heat allows the water to swish around the bowl to give it a quick clean. If the bowl is very greasy, wash it by hand. This takes about 10 minutes. However, it's just as easy to remove the bowl and place it in the dishwasher; it always comes out gleaming. The lid is a little trickier to clean, so follow the manufacturer's guidelines, but whatever you do, don't immerse the lid in water.

Eat yourself healthy

Healthy eating means going back to basics. If you use fresh ingredients in at least 80 per cent of your diet, you will achieve better health. It is common sense after all. Food that has been put together in a factory is going to have fewer nutrients than 'pure' food. Your health is so important, and it is only when we get older that we really appreciate this.

My biggest concern is for our children. Without good, healthy foundations in place, they are more likely to develop ill health sooner than previous generations. Health problems associated with being overweight or obese cost the NHS more than £5 billion every year, and this is estimated to double by 2050. Parents are getting accustomed to seeing obese children so they are becoming less aware of their own child's weight problems. A study by Peninsula College of Medicine & Dentistry in Plymouth revealed that three-quarters of parents failed to recognise their child was overweight. 33 per cent of mothers and 57 per cent of fathers considered their child's weight to be 'about right' when, in fact, they were obese.

Are you getting enough?

We need to eat at least five portions of fruit and vegetables every day. We are all aware of the government healthy eating campaign, but do we really understand what it means and why it is so important? I recently did a workshop at a primary school and was horrified to find that the teacher thought five a day was a maximum! Five fruit and vegetables a day is actually the *minimum* we should consume. Please ignore adverts that claim that eating a chewy bar counts towards one of your five a day: this is simply not true. There is no way a chewy bar contains the same nutrients and phytonutrients found in fruit or vegetables.

Did you know? *Potatoes do not count as part of your five a day.*

What counts as a portion?

1 medium fruit, such as an apple, pear, orange or banana
2 small fruits, such as a satsuma, kiwi or plum
Half a large fruit, such as a melon, grapefruit or pineapple
30g of dried fruit
4 heaped tablespoons of green vegetables
3 heaped tablespoons of cooked vegetables, such as carrots or peas
3 heaped tablespoons of pulses or beans (baked beans do count!)
150ml of unsweetened fruit or vegetable juice (more than this quantity

won't add towards your five a day)
250ml of 100% fruit or vegetable smoothies count as two portions

Why do we need a minimum of five a day?
Fruit and vegetables contain vitamins and minerals as well as essential phytonutrients, which help protect you from diseases such as cancer and heart disease. They contain fibre, to keep your bowel healthy and happy, and they also help create a balanced diet.

Portion sizes
Many people tend to overload their plate with food and consequently overeat. Try using a smaller plate and you will soon be cutting calories without even noticing. Use the same principle when feeding your children – they often feel intimidated by an overloaded plate. Far better to give them less and enjoy hearing them ask for more than watch them struggle with a large meal.

Chew your food
Digestion starts when food enters your mouth, and chewing is a vital part of the digestive process. Chew your food slowly and enjoy the taste. Giving yourself time to eat will allow you to start hearing your body telling you when you've had enough. If you eat too fast, you stop listening to the signal from your brain telling you that you are full.

Sit at a table, not in front of the TV
This is not about etiquette. Your digestion will work better if you are sitting comfortably at a table, plus your attention will be on your food. Paul McKenna ran an interesting experiment by feeding unsuspecting cinema-goers with stale popcorn. No one noticed what it tasted like as they were too busy watching the film, and they all finished their large tubs. The idea is conscious eating – if you are aware of every mouthful, you are less likely to make bad food choices, less likely to binge and more likely to listen to your body when it tells you its full.

Get active
Dump the remote, hide the car keys and do all you can to keep moving. Not only are you burning calories, you're also increasing your heart rate, expanding your lungs and moving your muscles. Try to be more active during the day, as a slow metabolism holds on to weight. If you exercise in the hour prior to eating, your metabolic rate is higher, which means that any calories taken in will be burnt off quicker. Activity will not only help you shed pounds, it will also help strengthen your heart. Aim for at least 20 minutes a day. Try swimming, walking, cycling or even join a dancing class.

Whatever you choose, make sure you have fun.

Get hydrated

Many people confuse thirst signals for hunger pangs. Drink plenty of water (not fizzy drinks, tea or coffee!). This will help rehydrate you and will also keep hunger and headaches at bay.

Ditch the frying pan

Grill or oven-bake instead of frying your foods. If you love chips, try baking potato wedges coated with paprika and sprayed with olive oil for a healthier option. I fill a spray container with light olive oil, ready to spray food or pans, as this works well and reduces the oil content. If you want a healthier oil option choose coconut oil – it has amazing health-promoting properties and has also been shown to aid weight loss.

Colour therapy

You can tell at a glance whether a meal is healthy or not. Healthy food is full of colour and vibrancy; junk food is biscuit-coloured. Fill your plate with a variety of colours for a healthy and nutritious meal. You can choose your food by its colour – with side vegetables, for example, you could opt for green cabbage, vibrant orange carrots and yellow sweetcorn. Get creative with your food colour palette.

Don't skip meals

Eat three nourishing meals a day. It is a complete myth that you will lose weight if you skip meals. All you will do is get a slump in your blood-sugar levels, get headaches and generally feel grotty... all the more reason to grab the nearest chocolate bar and wallow in self-pity. Instead, eat more, but choose your food with care. Pack all your meals with nutritious wholegrains to avoid sugar slumps and cravings. Organisations such as Slimming World and Weight Watchers include foods that are point-free or free to eat with their diets. These are usually fruits, vegetables and wholegrains, so there is no excuse, even when losing weight, to go hungry.

Smile!

Smiling and laughing increases production of feel-good endorphins. Not only will you feel better and more positive, but those around you will also benefit, as smiling is contagious.

Go green

Ditch the caffeine and opt for the healthier substitute. Start by switching to decaffeinated teas and coffees, but for ultimate health, cut down or ditch them altogether. Green tea is packed with powerful antioxidants, which can help lower cholesterol, boost your immune system and lower blood pressure. Caffeine does increase the heart rate and some say it helps speed up the metabolism to help you burn fat faster, but it can also have lots of detrimental health effects, including fluctuations in your blood-sugar levels, which can have you reaching for the nearest chocolate bar, so I would keep it to a minimum.

Cut the fizz

Fizzy drinks are packed with sugars and chemicals – even diet or sugar-free drinks are bad for you. If you like the fizz, try sparkling water mixed with fruit juice or natural cordial, or even better, a slice of lemon.

Avoid fast food

Fast food, junk food, processed food – they are all the same thing. These are packed with unhealthy fats, salts, sugars, chemicals and very few nutrients. They also cost more than home-cooked meals. So why do they account for approximately 70 to 80 per cent of the average family food shopping? Change your processed food habits and opt for easy-to-make, home-cooked meals.

Time for you

Step out of the rat race and find some time in your busy life. Set aside some time every day just for you, even for only five minutes. This could be reading, relaxing, a pampering session or just enjoying your favourite hobby. It may sound like a simple thing to do, but how often do you actually have time to yourself?

Respect your food

Learn to treat your food with respect and to get the most out of it. Food processing and cooking can destroy nutrients. Therefore, buy fresh ingredients and make home-cooked meals. Think about how you can get the most benefit from your food.

Nutrients, particularly vitamins, are lost when you boil vegetables. Buy a steamer to ensure your vegetables are packed with nutrients. They will taste better too. Invest in a wok and stir-fry to lock in flavours and nutrients. Slow cookers are also a great tool, not just for convenience, but also for making nutrient-rich soups, casseroles and one-pot meals. Raw foods are also good for you. These include salads, smoothies, juices or simply eating some fresh fruit or vegetable sticks.

Back to school
Hobbies can improve you mental and physical health. Learn to cook, exercise or even knit (known to lower blood pressure). It will also help build confidence and make friends.

Emotional health
One of the biggest reasons we overeat is emotional stress (the other big reason is boredom!). Be aware of your emotions. Vitamin B supplementation and St John's wort can help ease stress and depression. Unhealthy diets, particularly those including lots of processed foods, can upset your natural balance and can often lead to emotional health problems. Swapping to a nutrient-rich diet, while adding some interim supplementation, should really help.

Look after your teeth
Good teeth help you look younger and healthier. Have regular check-ups with your dentist. Brush and floss teeth twice a day to avoid gum disease – the major cause of losing your teeth. Some research suggests that flossing your teeth daily can help you live longer!

Sleep
Yes, sleep is one of the best health-promoting activities. Aim for a good eight hours' sleep a night. During sleep your body maintains its own glucose and insulin levels, as well as growth hormone levels, which is why you don't wake up during the night craving a tasty snack. Disturbed sleep not only makes you grumpy but can have a serious effect on your metabolism. Shift workers, particularly those who vary their shift patterns, can suffer more from weight fluctuations and mental health problems.

Teach your children well
This is the most important legacy you can ever leave your children. Teach them to enjoy, respect and know their food. Start them young by feeding them wholesome foods as soon as they are weaned. Children don't need specially formulated kids' foods, or tempting with cartoon characters. They just need to learn to love food for what it is. They will emulate their parents, so if you love good food, they will too.

Food swaps for health

This chapter details the everyday items you can swap to achieve a healthier lifestyle without noticing too much of a change.

Sugar

I would urge anyone wanting to lose weight or maintain a healthier lifestyle to try to substitute sugar wherever possible. Do not use artificial sweeteners; I personally have concerns about the high chemical content of artificial sweeteners and the mounting health concerns surrounding aspartame. Instead, opt for natural sweeteners. As your tastes change, you will start to notice natural sweetness from fruits and not be so reliant on excessive sugar hits. Reducing sugar will help lower your blood sugar and prevent gradual weight gain. People have reported a reduction in sugar cravings by taking a daily supplement of chromium as it helps balance blood sugar.

Did you know? Dates dramatically raise your blood sugar levels: one date has the same effect on your blood sugar as eating a whole punnet of raspberries!

• **Xylitol** This natural sweetener is low GI (glycaemic index) and has been shown to reduce gum disease and cavities. It also comes under the name of Perfect Sweet and is available from health food stores and some leading supermarkets.
• **Sweet Freedom natural sweetener and syrups** These contain just three ingredients: apples, grapes and carob. They contain 25 per cent fewer calories than sugar and you need around one-third less gram for gram. They are low GL (glycaemic load) and great for all the family, from dieters to diabetics alike, and kids love the taste. They are available from supermarkets and health food shops. Agave syrup is also low GI.
• **Stevia** Stevia rebaudiana bertoni, commonly known as stevia, is a wild plant from the subtropical forest in North-East Paraguay. The leaves of stevia contain glycosides, of which sweetening power is between 250 and 400 times their equivalent in sugar. The stevia leaf contains numerous phytonutrients and trace minerals and is diabetic safe. It has been available worldwide for many years but was only launched in the UK in December 2011. The only problem when switching to stevia is to know how much to use as it is so much sweeter than sugar. I prefer to use xylitol in recipes as it can be used as a direct swap for sugar, so measurements remain the same.

SWAP SUGAR FOR
xylitol, natural sweeteners, stevia or fruit.

Did you know? In the UK there are 2.8 million individuals currently diagnosed with diabetes, but there are also more than 5.5 million being treated for obesity.

Salt

Most people consume far too much salt (sodium) in their diet. The maximum daily allowance is 6g per day. This is just over 1 teaspoon per day, so think about that when you randomly add salt in your cooking or pile it over your food. Remember, sodium is in most junk or processed foods, so in order to cut down, opt for home-cooked equivalents. Excess salt leads to high blood pressure, some cancers, including stomach cancer, osteoporosis and heart disease. If you would like to start reducing your salt intake gradually, opt for something like Solo low-sodium salt, which contains 60 per cent less sodium than salt but is also packed with other great minerals such as magnesium.

SWAP SALT FOR
natural herbs and spices, or reduced-sodium salt.

Oil

As much as the media like to push fat-free diets, we do need to have good fats/oils in our diet for optimum health. Swapping vegetable oil for olive oil is a good start, giving you Omega-9, but for added health benefits I would recommend switching to coconut oil. It can be purchased in jars and will remain solid at room temperature but will melt quickly with cooking. Although the oil does smell coconut-y, it does not transfer to the food. Coconut oil has a vast number of health benefits, as well as being beneficial when using topically on the hair or skin. It has also been shown to help with weight loss. The real benefits of oils come when you start to use Omega-3-rich oils such as flax oil. You can only use flax cold (as heating destroys the nutrients), so why not swap olive oil for flax oil when making a dressing or cold dip such as houmous or salsa. You can also get Omega-3 by eating oily fish such as mackerel, herring, tuna, salmon and sardines, from seeds such as pumpkin and flax, and walnuts. Omega-6 comes from sunflower, pumpkin and sesame seeds, and oils such as evening primrose, safflower and soya. The real baddies are transfats – most commonly described in labelling as hydrogenated fats. You will find these in most processed or junk foods, so always read the labels and try to avoid them.

SWAP OILS AND FATS FOR
seeded oils such as coconut oil, flax oil, oily fish and seeds.

Milk

We all know we shouldn't opt for full-fat milk. Instead use skimmed milk. You could also try soya milk (this works fine for cooking most things, though it does curdle in tea and coffee). Rice and oat milks are also available, though more expensive options.

SWAP FULL-FAT MILK FOR
skimmed or soya milk.

Cream

Cream is used in many recipes or to accompany desserts. Opt instead for low-fat crème fraîche, low-fat natural yoghurt (I use Total 0% in cooking), low-fat cream cheese or, the lowest-fat option of them all, quark. Quark can taste a bit odd on its own, so if you are using it to replace cream in a dessert, mix it with a little vanilla essence and some low-fat crème fraîche. For added sweetness you could stir in a little Sweet Freedom syrup.

SWAP CREAM FOR
low-fat crème fraîche, fat-free Greek yoghurt, low-fat cream cheese, or quark.

Chocolate

We all love chocolate, but avoid the extra-sweet confectionery made with dairy milk. For those serious about health, opt instead for dark chocolate, ideally with a cocoa content of at least 70 per cent. A little goes a long way and yes, you will soon adjust to the taste and wonder how you could have ever eaten that sickly sweet Mars bar. I recommend Willie Harcourt's Pure Cacao. It is great in both sweet and savoury recipes. I am a huge fan, even more so as it is actually a very healthy product... chocolate and healthy – my type of food!

SWAP DAIRY MILK CHOCOLATE FOR
dark chocolate (at least 70 per cent cocoa solids).

Did you know? Catechins found in cocoa, tea and dark grapes protect against cardiovascular disease.

Ice cream

Everyone loves ice cream, but it is not particularly healthy, so try frozen yoghurt or make your own smoothies and freeze. Sorbets are very light and cleansing on the palate but can be very high in sugar.

SWAP ICE CREAM FOR
frozen yoghurt or frozen smoothies.

Refined carbohydrates

One of the biggest problems in modern diets is the high levels of refined carbohydrates, which basically translate as 'white stuff' (sugar, flour, pasta, bread, biscuits, cakes); the list is endless. These refined carbohydrates convert to glucose, raising blood-sugar levels (and contribute to an increased risk of diabetes). If an excessive quantity of carbohydrate is consumed and not 'burned off', they get converted to fat. Instead, swap to complex carbohydrates – these are foods that haven't been processed, such as wholewheat pasta, brown flour, wholegrains, cereals, nuts and seeds. They contain more nutrients and don't have the same negative effect as refined carbohydrates.

SWAP REFINED CARBOHYDRATES FOR
wholegrains, seeds, nuts and cereals.

Crisps

Crisps can be high in fat and salt and contain very few nutrients. If you fancy a savoury snack, pop your own popcorn. Corn kernels are cheap to buy and take minutes to pop. Kids also love watching them expand and pop in the pan.

SWAP CRISPS FOR
popcorn.

Fizzy drinks

Fizzy drinks contain high levels of sugar and caffeine and very few nutrients. Many professionals consider the high consumption of fizzy drinks to be one of the biggest causes of obesity, Type 2 diabetes and dental problems. The high consumption of 'diet' fizzy drinks has also been linked to mental health problems because of the artificial sweeteners. Most fizzy drinks also contain phosphoric acid, which can interfere with the body's ability to utilise calcium, leading to problems such as osteoporosis. The caffeine and cocktail of chemicals in fizzy drinks can also upset your natural stomach-acid balance, leading to gastrointestinal problems.

SWAP FIZZY DRINKS FOR
water, fresh juices and green tea.

Caffeine

We are becoming increasingly reliant on caffeine, believing it is going to give us a mental or physical boost to help us through the day. There has been a lot of publicity around the benefits of green coffee capsules and also raspberry ketones, which often come combined with caffeine to help stimulate the metabolism and aid weight loss. Be very careful when adding stimulants to your diet – I recommend seeking advice from a medical doctor or a qualified practitioner of nutrition.

SWAP CAFFEINE FOR
green coffee, dandelion coffee, green tea and herbal teas.

Cheese

Many of us love cheese, but did you know you can cut down on cheese for things like cheese sauces or even cheesy scrambled eggs by using a product called nutritional yeast flakes? These flakes are commonly used by vegans who want a cheesy flavour without the dairy, but they can be used by anyone. If you add a few tablespoons to a cheese sauce before adding the cheese, you can halve or more the amount of cheese needed. In addition, nutritional yeast flakes are packed with B vitamins. Remember, if you love cheese, swap to a low-fat version. There are now many great-tasting ones on the market. Also, if using Cheddar in cooking, opt for a mature Cheddar as you need less to create the flavour.

SWAP FULL-FAT CHEESE FOR
nutritional yeast flakes or low-fat cheese.

Breakfast like a king...

Breakfast really is the most important meal of the day. It is very true that your concentration and mental alertness are sluggish when you skip this essential meal. People often comment that they struggle to lose weight, yet eat very little. Breakfast is usually the one meal they avoid in a bid to reduce calories, but this results in the body hanging on to body fat and a tendency for the dieter to start snacking on inappropriate options mid-morning when hunger pangs become too strong to avoid.

Choose foods that are high in protein and fibre, lean protein sources such as lean ham or bacon. Opt for wholegrains such as wholemeal seeded breads and oats as these will keep you fuller for longer and help balance your blood-sugar levels, avoiding sugar slumps that could have you reaching for the nearest chocolate bar.

Did you know? *According to a study by the University of Aberdeen, there was a 25 per cent decrease in strokes for middle-aged volunteers who were given more wholegrains in their diet.*

Breakfast

It is so important to have a good breakfast every day. It is a complete myth that skipping this essential meal will help you lose weight – in fact, it is more likely to have the opposite effect. If you are concerned about your weight or want to increase your energy throughout the day, opt for foods that provide slow-release energy. These include wholegrains, pulses, oats and protein. Avoid sugary foods or refined carbohydrates as they will simply give you a sharp burst of energy, raising your blood sugar for a short period of time, but then dropping you down to feeling tired and sluggish within the hour.

Garlic and thyme grilled tomatoes

6 tomatoes, halved
2–3 cloves of garlic,
  peeled and
  roughly chopped
Few sprigs of thyme
Freshly ground
  black pepper
Spray of olive oil

I love these herby tomatoes: they are perfect for a delicious breakfast or brunch, or as a side dish for a savoury meal.

• Place the halved tomatoes, cut-side up, on a greased or non-stick baking tray.

• Sprinkle the garlic and thyme on top of each tomato half.

• Season with black pepper.

• Finish with a fine spray of olive oil.

• Place on the high rack and cook at 230°C for 8–10 minutes, or until the tomatoes start to soften.

• Serve immediately.

Did you know? *Tomatoes are rich in lycopene, a powerful antioxidant that has been shown to help reduce some cancers.*

Pan-roasted breakfast

Just because you're following a healthy diet doesn't mean you have to go without. Most people think that cooked breakfasts should be avoided, but this is a myth – a good breakfast will set you up for the day. Add some baked beans (the low-salt, low-sugar variety ideally) and you have a complete meal that will see you through till lunchtime. This dish is also suitable for supper, especially when you require comfort food.

• Place the tomatoes, garlic and bacon in an ovenproof dish. Drizzle with a little coconut oil or olive oil, and season with black pepper and thyme.

• Place on the high rack and cook at 200°C for 10 minutes.

• Remove from the oven. Make four even cavities in the mixture and crack an egg into each hole.

• Cover the dish with foil and bake for a further 10–15 minutes, until the eggs are cooked to your liking.

• Remove from the oven, sprinkle with the parsley, and serve immediately with wholemeal toast and baked beans.

Healthy swap! *If you don't want bacon, swap it for lean, freshly sliced ham.*

400g cherry
  tomatoes
3 cloves of garlic,
  peeled
8 rashers of thick,
  very lean bacon,
  fat removed,
  roughly chopped
1 tsp coconut oil or
  olive oil
Freshly ground
  black pepper
1–2 sprigs of thyme
4 large eggs
2 tbsp chopped
  parsley
Wholemeal toast
  and baked beans,
  to serve

Healthy breakfast kebabs

1–2 tbsp runny
  honey or agave
  syrup
3–4 tbsp orange
  juice
1 tsp ground
  cinnamon
  (optional)
4–6 dried figs
4–6 dried apricots
4–6 dates
4–6 prunes
Dried apple rings
1 banana, cut into
  2cm pieces
1 orange, peeled
  and segmented
Natural yoghurt, to
  serve

These fruity kebabs are perfect if you fancy something light and healthy for breakfast. Feel free to choose your own fruit combinations.

• In a bowl, mix the honey or agave syrup and orange juice together. Stir in the cinnamon, if using.

• Soak the dried fruit in the sweetened orange juice for at least 1 hour. Drain the fruit and reserve the juice.

• When ready to cook, alternately thread fresh and dried fruit pieces onto two skewers. (If you are using wooden skewers, pre-soak them.)

• Place the skewers on the grill rack.

• Set the temperature to 250°C and cook for 3–5 minutes on each side.

• Serve with a drizzle of the reserved honey and orange juice and a dollop of natural yoghurt.

Banana and blueberry toastie

Serves
1–2

1–2 slices of rye or
   wholemeal bread
1 large banana
1 tsp Sweet
   Freedom syrup
   (optional)
Sprinkle of ground
   cinnamon
Handful of fresh
   blueberries

So simple yet so delicious, this toastie does the job when you're craving something sweet. Makes a great breakfast or after-school snack too.

• Place the bread on the high rack, or grill rack if you have one. Set the temperature to the highest setting and grill or toast the bread for 2–3 minutes on one side.

• In the meantime, mash the banana with the syrup and cinnamon, to taste.

• Remove the bread from the oven, spread the banana mixture over the untoasted side and top with a sprinkle of berries.

• Return to the oven and grill for a further 2 minutes. Serve immediately.

Did you know? *A study in the USA has shown that eating one serving of blueberries per week can lower your risk of heart disease and high blood pressure by 10 per cent.*

Chive and onion corn bread

1 large onion,
peeled and finely
sliced
1 tsp coconut oil or
olive oil
350g fine polenta
2 tsp gluten-free
baking powder
1 tsp bicarbonate of
soda
Freshly ground
black pepper
1 tbsp freshly
chopped chives
(or 1 tsp dried
chives)
350g natural
yoghurt
2 eggs
275g creamed corn

If you fancy a gluten-free bread, this is really simple to make and tastes delicious. If you don't like onion, you could swap it for fresh herbs instead.

• Place the onion in an ovenproof dish. Drizzle with the coconut oil or olive oil.

• Place on the high rack and cook at 200°C for 10 minutes, until soft.

• Place all the dry ingredients, including the chives, in a bowl and combine well.

• In a separate bowl, mix the yoghurt, eggs and creamed corn together. Mix with the dry ingredients and the softened onion. Transfer to a greased 20–24cm round cake tin.

• Place on the high rack and cook at 180°C for 20–25 minutes. If the bread starts to brown too quickly, move it to the lower rack. Serve hot or cold.

Did you know? *Onions are packed with quercetin, a more potent antioxidant than vitamin E, which helps fight a variety of illnesses, ranging from the common cold and fatigue to colon, prostate and breast cancer.*

Baked ham and eggs

Serves

2

This is a great alternative to fried breakfast. Why not add some vine tomatoes with garlic and thyme, to roast while the ham and eggs are cooking?

2–4 slices of ham
3 eggs
200g low-fat crème
   fraîche
½ tsp dried parsley
Freshly ground
   black pepper

• Grease two individual pie dishes.

• Carefully line the dishes with the ham, making sure the slices overlap so the egg mixture can't leak through any gaps.

• Place the dishes on a baking tray – it will make it easier for you to manage once they are full of the egg mixture.

• In a bowl, mix the eggs with the crème fraîche and parsley. Season with black pepper.

• Pour the mixture into the dishes.

• Place on the low rack and cook at 200°C for 20 minutes, until the eggs are puffed up and golden.

• Serve immediately.

The healthy English

2–4 slices of lean
bacon, fat
removed

6–8 vine tomatoes
(or 2 large
tomatoes,
halved, if you
prefer)

6–8 mushrooms

Garlic-infused olive
oil

2–4 eggs

There really is nothing nicer than a full English, especially on a lazy weekend morning. This is a healthy version but still packs a punch. You can serve it with low-salt/low-sugar baked beans and wholemeal seeded bread.

• Boil the kettle. Meanwhile, put the bacon, tomatoes and mushrooms in an ovenproof dish. Brush the tomatoes and mushrooms with a little of the infused olive oil.

• Place on the high rack and grill at 235°C until the bacon is cooked to your liking. If you like really crispy bacon you may want to move the tomatoes and mushrooms to the lower rack or base of the halogen while the bacon crisps up.

• When the bacon has only a couple of minutes left to cook, place a saucepan filled with just-boiled water on the hob on high. Once it is bubbling, add the eggs one at a time to poach.

• While the eggs are cooking you can plate up the rest of the breakfast – adding your cooked baked beans and toast. Add the poached egg and sprinkle with black pepper.

• Serve immediately.

NB: If you're not confident poaching eggs, use poach pods (available from Lakeland) or line a cup with clingfilm and break the egg into the clingfilm. Scoop up the edges and scrunch to secure, so you end up with a pouch of egg. Drop into the boiling water and cook for 4–6 minutes, depending on how you like your eggs done.

Side Dishes

This chapter is packed with recipes to use as accompaniments, side dishes or in some cases you can have them on their own. Since my first halogen book was published I have received hundreds of emails from all around the world. It seems that you all want to know more about preparing and cooking side dishes and vegetables, so I hope this chapter helps. Remember, if you are using the halogen to cook your main meal as well, you may need to use the extension ring to create more space.

4 sweet potatoes,
scrubbed
$1/2$–1 chilli, finely
chopped
1–2 cloves of garlic,
peeled and finely
chopped
2 spring onions,
finely chopped
2–3 tbsp low-fat
cream cheese
Salt and freshly
ground black
pepper
Dash of milk
(optional)

Baked sweet potato and chilli

If you have never tasted a baked sweet potato, I urge you to give it a go; it really is delicious. A simple meal but very wholesome and healthy!

• Preheat the halogen oven to 180°C.

• Prick the potatoes all over with a sharp knife and place them on the lower rack.

• Bake the potatoes until they are soft in the middle with crunchy jackets. This normally takes around 45–60 minutes, depending on size.

• Meanwhile, mix the chilli, garlic, spring onions and cream cheese together in a bowl.

• When the potatoes are cooked, scoop out the flesh. Mix the potato with the cream cheese mixture and season to taste. Add a dash of milk if the mixture is too dry (it should be the consistency of mashed potato).

• Stuff the jackets with the mixture. Bake in the oven for 10–12 minutes until the tops are golden.

Did you know? Sweet potatoes are a great source of carotenoids. Studies show a diet rich in carotenoids can help protect you from cancer.

Baked new potatoes

This must be the simplest recipe of all!

• Preheat the halogen oven to 220°C.

• Place the potatoes in a bowl with the oil, garlic, herbs and paprika.

• Season to taste. Stir well, ensuring the potatoes are well coated.

• Tip the potatoes into a baking tray and place on the high rack.

• Bake for approximately 35–45 minutes, turning occasionally until golden. Simple!

1kg new potatoes, washed
Dash of coconut oil or olive oil
2–3 cloves of garlic, peeled and crushed
2–3 tsp mixed herbs (fresh or dried)
2–3 tsp paprika
Salt and freshly ground black pepper

Potato wedges

Potato wedges are a great substitute for deep-fried chips. These wedges are lower in fat than chips, so are a healthier option. Why not try this recipe using sweet potatoes instead, which go well with a sweet chilli dip. Lakeland sells a halogen oven (Visicook Crisp & Bake) with a rotating arm, which acts in a similar way to the Tefal Actifry. These machines are great because they require less fat.

Potatoes, cut into chunks
1 tbsp olive oil or coconut oil
1–2 tsp paprika

• Preheat the halogen oven to 210°C.

• Place the potato chunks in a bowl with the oil and paprika and toss to ensure the potatoes are evenly coated. If you want to cut down on fat, spray the potatoes with olive oil instead.

• Transfer to a baking tray or place in the bottom of the oven.

• Cook for 25–30 minutes until golden, turning occasionally.

Variation: Add chopped garlic, herbs of your choice and chillies for extra spice.

Garlic and rosemary roast potatoes

4 large potatoes
5–6 tbsp coconut
oil or olive oil
3–4 tsp semolina
1 bulb of garlic,
cloves peeled
1–2 red onions,
peeled and cut
into wedges
3–5 sprigs of
rosemary

I love the flavours of garlic and rosemary, and they go brilliantly with potatoes. You can use large potatoes, as described in this recipe, or mini new potatoes (with skins still on). If using new potatoes, you won't need to steam or boil them, or use semolina. Simply add them to the dish with the garlic, onions and rosemary, and toss in a little coconut oil or olive oil.

• Peel and cut the potatoes into wedges.

• Steam or boil the potatoes for 10 minutes.

• Meanwhile, preheat the halogen oven to 200°C.

• Add the oil to a 1cm-deep roasting tin and place on the high rack.

• Drain the potatoes but keep them in the saucepan.

• Sprinkle the semolina on the potatoes.

• Cover the pan and shake the potatoes for a few seconds.

• Carefully remove the hot roasting tin from the halogen. Add the potatoes to the hot oil, being careful not to splash (I use tongs to do this).

• Add the garlic, onion wedges and rosemary, ensuring they are evenly distributed around the potatoes.

• Roast for 40 minutes, turning regularly to ensure an even, crisp coating. Drain the fat and cook for a further 30 minutes, until the potatoes are crisp and golden.

Low-fat dauphinoise potatoes

*I love Dauphinoise potatoes but if they are made with
cream they can be very calorific. This recipe uses fat-free
Greek yoghurt and quark.*

• Preheat the halogen oven to 200°C or use the preheat
setting.

• In a bowl, mix the crème fraîche or quark, yoghurt
and milk until thoroughly combined. Season with
nutmeg, salt and black pepper.

• Grease an ovenproof dish, then add a layer of potato
slices followed by a little garlic and some onion slices.

• Place a little of the crème fraîche mixture on top
(leaving the majority to pour over the top layer) and
cover with another layer of potatoes.

• Continue the layers, finishing with the crème fraîche
and a sprinkling of Parmesan, if using. Season with
black pepper.

• Place on the low rack and cook for 50–60 minutes,
until the potatoes are cooked through. If they start to
look too dark on top, cover with foil.

250ml low-fat
    crème fraîche or
    quark
250ml fat-free
    Greek yoghurt
50ml milk
Nutmeg, grated
Salt and freshly
    ground black
    pepper
500g potatoes,
    peeled and very
    finely sliced
2–4 cloves of garlic,
    peeled and
    crushed
1 onion, peeled and
    finely sliced
Grated Parmesan
    cheese (optional)

Sweet potato, chilli and coriander nests

4–5 sweet potatoes,
   peeled and diced
1/2 tbsp low-fat
   spread
Dash of milk
Freshly ground
   black pepper
1–2 fresh chillies,
   finely chopped
3 spring onions,
   finely chopped
Small handful of
   fresh coriander
   leaves, finely
   chopped

I am a big fan of sweet potatoes. Here I season them with butter and black pepper to create these delicious mash nests – very retro!

• Place the diced potatoes in a steamer and cook until soft, for 15–25 minutes, depending on the size of the pieces.

• Mash with the low-fat spread and milk, and season with black pepper to taste. If you like a smooth mash, use a potato ricer or an electric hand mixer (though roughly mash the potatoes first, otherwise you may buckle the mixer blades).

• Stir in the chillies, spring onions and coriander leaves.

• Preheat the halogen oven to 180°C or use the preheat setting.

• Transfer the mash to a piping bag. On a very well-greased or lined baking tray, pipe 4–5cm round nests. Start at the centre and pipe round, slightly overlapping the inner lines. Pipe a line of mash on top of the outer edge to form a wall to the nests.

• Place the tray on the low rack and cook for 15 minutes. You can serve these as they are, or you can fill the nests with crumbled goat's cheese or low-fat feta cheese. Once filled, return to the oven for a further 5–10 minutes, until the cheese has melted.

Did you know? *Sweet potatoes are a great source of carotenoids and vitamin A, which can help boost your immune system.*

Homemade sweet potato chips

Who can resist chips? These are made using spray oil (I place olive oil in a spray container as this works out cheaper than buying a spray oil). Using oil in this way cuts down on the amount of fat in the chips, so this can be a guilt-free indulgence.

3–4 large potatoes, sliced into chips
Olive oil spray
Paprika
Fresh or dried chilli flakes
Sea salt

• Preheat the halogen oven to 220°C or use the preheat setting.

• Steam or boil the potatoes for 5 minutes.

• Meanwhile, spray a baking tray with olive oil. Drain the potatoes and place on the baking tray in a single layer. Spray with a little more olive oil and sprinkle with paprika (this helps to create a golden colour and nice flavour).

• Place on the high rack and bake for 10–15 minutes before turning over, spraying again and adding the chilli flakes. Cook for a further 10–15 minutes, or until the chips are cooked. (The cooking times depend on the thickness of the chips.)

• Serve sprinkled with sea salt and more chilli flakes if liked.

Bombay sweet potatoes

2 tbsp coconut oil
or olive oil

4–6 sweet potatoes,
peeled and diced

2 cloves of garlic,
peeled and
crushed

2cm piece of
ginger, peeled
and grated

$1/2$ tsp turmeric

1 chilli, finely diced

$1/2$ tsp chilli powder

1 tsp garam masala

1 tsp cumin seeds

$1/2$ tsp ground
coriander

Juice and zest of
$1/2$ lemon

Sweet potatoes go so brilliantly with spices, and this Bombay potato recipe works a treat. Serve as an accompaniment to your favourite curry. I love to serve these with a soup or salad to add a bit of heat to the meal.

• Put the oil in an ovenproof dish. If using coconut oil, melt on a medium heat for 1–2 minutes in the halogen.

• Put the sweet potatoes in the dish and toss in the oil to coat.

• Mix the garlic and spices together with the lemon zest. Sprinkle onto the sweet potatoes and toss well. Squeeze the lemon juice over the potatoes and combine again.

• Place on the high rack and cook at 200°C for 20–25 minutes, until the potatoes are soft, turning halfway through cooking.

• Serve immediately.

Broccoli gratin

This is a lovely accompaniment to a roast, or have it as a simple supper with some ham. Nutritional yeast flakes give this dish a cheesy flavour without the added fat. You can buy yeast flakes, which are a rich source of B vitamins, from health food stores.

• Steam the broccoli until it is just soft – you don't want to overcook it.

• Meanwhile, mix the yoghurt, cream cheese and milk together in a bowl. Season to taste and stir in the nutritional yeast flakes, if using.

• In a separate bowl, combine the breadcrumbs, oats and Parmesan. Season to taste.

• Place the broccoli in an ovenproof dish. Pour over the creamed mixture, then sprinkle the breadcrumb mix on top.

• Place on the low rack and cook at 180°C for 10–15 minutes.

• Serve piping hot.

Did you know? An enzyme in broccoli has been found to help fight breast cancer and prostate cancer.

---

1 head of broccoli, cut into florets
3 tbsp Greek yoghurt
2 tbsp low-fat cream cheese
3 tbsp skimmed milk
Salt and freshly ground black pepper
2–3 tbsp nutritional yeast flakes (optional)
3 tbsp wholemeal breadcrumbs
1 tbsp oats
1 tbsp grated Parmesan cheese (optional)

Spicy roasted sweet potato with yoghurt dressing

3 sweet potatoes,
    peeled and diced
2 red onions,
    peeled and
    quartered
2–4 cloves of garlic,
    peeled and
    roughly chopped
Drizzle of coconut
    oil or olive oil
1 chilli, finely
    chopped
3cm piece of fresh
    ginger, peeled
    and grated
2 tsp coriander
    seeds, crushed
2 tsp cumin seeds,
    crushed
1 tsp turmeric
Salt and freshly
    ground black
    pepper
Handful of fresh
    coriander leaves,
    chopped
2–3 tbsp thick
    yoghurt (I prefer
    Greek Total
    yoghurt)

Sweet potatoes work brilliantly with spicy flavours as they seem to absorb the spices so well. The yoghurt dressing helps soothe the palate after the fire of the spices. Add more chillies if you like it more spicy, but remove the chilli seeds if you want to avoid too much heat.

● Preheat the halogen oven to 200°C.

● Put the sweet potatoes, onions and garlic in an ovenproof dish. Drizzle over the oil and toss to coat.

● Place on the low rack and cook for 10 minutes.

● Meanwhile, mix the spices together in a small bowl and season to taste.

● Once the 10 minutes are up, lift the lid of the halogen and sprinkle the spices over the vegetables. Carefully toss to coat. If necessary, add a little more oil, but the vegetables should not be soaked in oil, just lightly coated.

● Cook for a further 15–20 minutes, until the potatoes are soft.

● Remove from the oven and transfer to a serving dish. Sprinkle over the coriander and serve with a dollop of yoghurt.

Did you know? Sweet potatoes are a great source of carotenoids and vitamin A, which help keep your respiratory tract healthy.

Mediterranean-style roasted vegetables

This is a really easy dish that can be eaten with feta or goat's cheese, used as a pasta sauce or even as a pizza topping.

• Mix the vegetables and garlic in a bowl or if, like me, you hate washing up, you can do this directly in the ovenproof dish.

• In a small bowl, mix a drizzle of oil with the balsamic vinegar, sugar, oregano and seasoning. Pour this over the vegetables and toss well, ensuring the vegetables are evenly coated in the oil mixture.

• Place on the low rack and cook at 200°C for 20–30 minutes, until the vegetables are soft.

• To serve, sprinkle with the herbs and a little crumbled goat's cheese or low-fat feta.

Did you know? *Tomatoes are a great source of carotenoid lycopene, which has been shown to help reduce cholesterol.*

---

2 red onions, peeled and quartered
1 aubergine, thickly sliced
2 courgettes, thickly sliced
8–12 vine tomatoes
2 red peppers, quartered
3–4 cloves of garlic, peeled and roughly chopped
Coconut oil or olive oil
Dash of balsamic vinegar
1 tsp granulated sugar or xylitol
2 tsp dried oregano
Salt and freshly ground black pepper
Fresh oregano, basil and thyme, and low-fat feta, to serve

Baked fennel

1–2 fennel bulbs,
cut into wedges
Coconut oil or olive
oil
1–2 cloves of garlic,
peeled and
chopped
Salt and freshly
ground black
pepper

Fennel is a really underrated vegetable. It has a lovely flavour and goes well with fish dishes, as well as vegetarian or meat dishes. This is a really simple side dish.

• Place the fennel in a pan of boiling water and simmer gently for 10 minutes. Drain and place in an oiled ovenproof dish.

• Drizzle with coconut oil or olive oil, add the garlic and season.

• Place on the medium rack and cook at 190°C for 20–25 minutes.

• Serve with a drizzle of extra-virgin olive oil.

Did you know? *Fennel features prominently in Mediterranean cuisine. It is a good source of niacin, calcium, iron and magnesium, and an excellent source of dietary fibre, vitamin C, folic acid, potassium and manganese.*

Garlic courgettes

2 tsp coconut oil or
olive oil
3–4 cloves of garlic,
peeled and finely
chopped
4–5 courgettes,
thickly sliced
Very generous
sprinkling of
coarse-milled
black pepper

This is a lovely side dish but it makes a delicious salad combined with rocket leaves, finely sliced red onion and black pepper.

• Place the oil in an ovenproof dish. If using coconut oil, place on the high rack at 220°C and melt for no more than 1 minute.

• Add the garlic and courgettes and toss well in the oil.

• Season generously with black pepper.

• Cook for 8–12 minutes until soft and golden.

• Serve immediately.

Antioxidant-rich baked butternut squash

*This simple yet very nutritious dish is packed full of
antioxidants and is suitable for vegans. It's a healthy option
on its own, or serve it as a side dish.*

• Cut the butternut squash in half lengthways. Scoop
out the flesh and dice, leaving the shell of the squash
intact.

• Try to keep the diced vegetables all the same size.
Place the diced squash on a baking tray alongside the
sweet potato, onion, red pepper, half the garlic and
chilli, and all the tomatoes. Add a sprig of thyme.
Drizzle with coconut oil or olive oil and season with
black pepper.

• Brush the lining of the squash casings with coconut
oil or olive oil. Place the remaining half of the garlic
and chilli in the casings. Add a sprig of thyme in each
and season with black pepper.

• Place the squash shells on the low rack and cook at
200°C for 20 minutes.

• Remove and place the squash shells on the base of
the halogen. Place the high rack on top and add the
tray with the remaining vegetables. Cook for 20
minutes.

• Meanwhile, combine the oats, breadcrumbs and
herbs in a small bowl.

• Remove the shells and vegetables. Combine the
vegetables with the diced feta and place in the shells.

• Sprinkle with the oat mixture.

• Return to the oven on the high rack for 10 minutes
before serving.

1 butternut squash
1 sweet potato,
    peeled and diced
1 large red onion,
    peeled and cut
    into wedges
1 red pepper, cut
    into wedges
2–3 cloves of garlic,
    peeled and
    roughly chopped
1 red chilli
    (deseeded if you
    don't want it too
    hot)
4–6 cherry or vine
    tomatoes
3 sprigs of thyme
2 tbsp coconut oil
    or olive oil
Freshly ground
    black pepper
2 tbsp oats
3 slices of
    wholemeal bread,
    whizzed into
    breadcrumbs
1 tsp mixed herbs
80g low-fat feta
    cheese, diced
    (optional)

1 red cabbage,
finely shredded
1 large apple,
peeled and diced
1 small red onion,
peeled and finely
chopped
1 tsp allspice
250ml red wine
vinegar

Red cabbage

Serve this hot as a vegetable side dish (perfect at Christmas too!) or store in sterilised jars.

• Place all the ingredients in a saucepan and gently bring to the boil. Cook for 10 minutes and then transfer to a casserole or ovenproof dish.

• Secure a double layer of foil over the top to form a lid.

• Place on the low rack and cook at 160°C for 1–1^1/$_2$ hours until soft.

• Serve hot or cold.

Did you know? *Anthocyanins found in blueberries, blackberries, purple plums, red wine, red cabbage and aubergines protect the immune system against viral and bacterial infection.*

Savoury vegetable rice

I love rice dishes but some people are not confident cooking rice. On the hob I simply boil for 5 minutes, pop on a lid and remove from the heat to stand for 10 minutes – I get perfect rice every time. You can cook rice in the halogen oven too. Follow these simple steps and you can then adapt this basic principle to make your own variations.

• Place the coconut oil in a sauté pan. Add the spring onions, garlic, red and yellow peppers, and celery and cook for 5 minutes to soften.

• Add all the remaining ingredients, along with 600ml water, and gently bring to the boil.

• Transfer to a casserole or deep ovenproof dish. Cover with a double layer of foil.

• Place on the low rack and cook at 190°C for 10–15 minutes.

• Fluff with a fork and serve immediately.

Did you know? *Sweetcorn contains lutein and zeaxanthin, and is high in thiamine (vitamin B1) and folic acid.*

---

1 tsp coconut oil
4–5 spring onions, finely chopped
2 cloves of garlic, peeled and finely chopped
1 red pepper, diced
1 yellow pepper, diced
1 stick of celery, diced
50g frozen peas
50g frozen or tinned sweetcorn
250g basmati rice
1 bay leaf

Roasted spiced cauliflower

1 large head of
 cauliflower,
 separated into
 florets
1 white onion,
 peeled and finely
 diced
1 tbsp coconut oil
 or olive oil
2–3 tbsp curry
 powder
Small handful of
 fresh coriander,
 to garnish

*I like to serve cauliflower with a selection of Indian dishes,
such as lentil dahl (see p. 150) and Bombay sweet potatoes
(see p.32). Make sure the cauliflower is completely dry
before you toss it in the oil. I use coconut oil but if you don't
have any you can use olive oil instead.*

• Place the cauliflower florets and onion in a bowl.
Toss in the melted coconut oil or olive oil until evenly
covered.

• Place the cauliflower on a greased baking tray.
Sprinkle with the curry powder and gently toss to
cover all the florets.

• Place on the low rack and cook at 190°C for 15–20
minutes until roasted and quite soft. Make sure the
cauliflower still holds its form and has a slight bite to it
though – you don't want soggy cauliflower!

• Garnish with freshly chopped coriander and serve
immediately.

Salads

We all need to eat more fruit and vegetables, and it is a great health benefit to combine both cooked and raw vegetables in your diet. Salads are a great way to increase the nutrient content of your meal, but I am not thinking of a bit of iceberg lettuce, tomato and cucumber. Think a combination of salad leaves, a selection of fruit and vegetables such as grated carrots, grapes, apple, oranges, beetroot and peppers – the combinations are endless. Try to make salads as vibrant and colourful as possible – the healthiest foods are always coloured.

Roasted red onion, beetroot and pepper salad with pine nuts

75g pine nuts
3 red onions,
    peeled and cut
    into wedges
2 beetroots, peeled
    and cut into
    wedges
2 red peppers, cut
    into wedges
Olive oil spray
Salt and freshly
    ground black
    pepper
Balsamic vinegar
2 tbsp extra-virgin
    olive oil
Mixed salad leaves

This is my favourite salad – if I am feeling really extravagant I might add a little crumbled goat's cheese!

• Place the pine nuts on a baking tray and spread them out. Place on the high rack (the grill rack preferably) and set the temperature to its highest setting. Roast for a couple of minutes until they start to brown. Be careful as they can catch very quickly. Remove and set aside.

• Place the onions, beetroots and red peppers on a baking tray, spray with olive oil, season and drizzle with balsamic vinegar. Preheat the halogen oven to 200°C. Place on the low rack and bake for 20–30 minutes.

• In a small bowl, make a dressing by mixing the extra-virgin olive oil with 1 tbsp of balsamic vinegar. Season to taste.

• Remove the roasted vegetables from the oven.

• Place the salad leaves on four serving plates and top with the roasted vegetables.

• Sprinkle with the pine nuts and finish with a drizzle of the dressing.

• Serve immediately.

Did you know? *Beetroot is not just a great blood purifier. It is also known to be high in potassium. Potassium is vital for a healthy body, and is especially helpful in maintaining a balanced blood pressure.*

Chorizo salad

I am a big fan of paprika so it comes as no surprise to hear I also love chorizo. When cooking, chorizo oozes a lovely red oil which looks as good as it tastes.

• Place the sliced chorizo and the coconut oil in an ovenproof dish.

• Place on the high rack and cook at 235°C for 5–10 minutes, stirring occasionally to ensure an even cook.

• Once the chorizo is cooked, remove with a slotted spoon, retaining the oils in the dish. Set the chorizo aside.

• Add the olive oil and the seeds to the dish. Cook for a further 2 minutes, stirring occasionally.

• Remove from the oven and leave to cool slightly.

• Place the salad leaves in a serving dish and stir in the onion and chorizo.

• Pour over the oil and seeds and serve immediately.

200g sliced chorizo
$^1/_2$ tsp coconut oil
1 tbsp olive oil
2 tbsp mixed seeds
100g rocket, watercress and spinach salad leaves (peppery leaves are a must!)
1 red onion, peeled and very finely chopped

Did you know? *Seed mix containing flax, sunflower and pumpkin seeds helps provide vitamins E and B, folic acid, manganese, magnesium and Omega-3 and 6.*

Warm vegetable salad with Puy lentils and goat's cheese

2 red onions,
peeled and cut
into wedges
1 red pepper, cut
into thick slices
1 yellow pepper, cut
into thick slices
2 sweet potatoes,
skin on and cut
into thick slices
1 courgette, sliced
10 cherry tomatoes
Olive oil
Salt and freshly
ground black
pepper
100g Puy lentils
2–3 sprigs of
rosemary
100g goat's cheese,
crumbled

Puy lentils are seriously underrated. If you haven't tried them, I urge you to give them a go – their slightly nutty flavour works so well with the roasted vegetables and goat's cheese.

• Place the vegetables in an ovenproof dish. Drizzle with olive oil and season.

• Place on the high rack and cook at 200°C for 20–30 minutes, until soft and roasted.

• Meanwhile, place the lentils in a saucepan. Cover with water and add the rosemary. Bring to the boil and cook for 15–20 minutes. Drain, discard the rosemary and place in a large serving dish or four individual dishes.

• Remove the vegetables from the oven and tip them over the lentils.

• Sprinkle with the crumbled goat's cheese.

• Serve immediately.

Did you know? *Rosemary has been shown to have energising effects.*

Grilled asparagus and poached egg salad

Serves

2

There is nothing better than British asparagus when in season – it goes so well with egg, but make sure you slightly undercook the eggs as you want oozing yolks. Yum!

• Place the asparagus on a baking tray. Drizzle with coconut oil or olive oil and season with black pepper.

• Place on the grill rack (see p.3), set the temperature to 250°C and cook for 8–10 minutes.

• Meanwhile, bring a pan of water to the boil and garnish two plates with the salad leaves.

• Approximately 3–4 minutes before the asparagus is ready, poach the eggs.

• Remove the asparagus from the oven, and place over the salad leaves.

• Top with the poached eggs and finish with some Parmesan shavings, black pepper and a drizzle of your favourite salad dressing.

250g asparagus
Coconut oil or olive oil
Freshly ground black pepper
80g salad leaves
2 eggs
Parmesan cheese
Salad dressing

Roasted beetroot and red pepper salad

500g baby
beetroots, peeled
and halved
2–3 red peppers,
quartered
Coconut oil or olive
oil
2–3 sprigs of
rosemary
100g rocket leaves
1 large red onion,
peeled and diced
2–3 tbsp olive oil
2 tbsp red wine
vinegar
Salt and freshly
ground black
pepper

If you have never had beetroot, I urge you to try this salad. Forget the bitter, vinegary beetroot you buy in a jar, this is totally different. The sweetness of the roasted beetroot combines well with the peppery salad leaves. Add some crumbled low-fat feta for a creamy contrast.

• Place the beetroots and red peppers on a baking tray. Drizzle with a little coconut oil or olive oil, ensuring the vegetables are evenly coated.

• Add some sprigs of rosemary.

• Place on the medium rack and cook at 180°C for 30–40 minutes until soft.

• Meanwhile, toss together the rocket and onion in a large serving dish.

• In a small bowl, mix the olive oil, vinegar and seasoning. Combine, adjusting the vinegar and olive oil to taste.

• When the beetroots and peppers are done, you can either leave them to cool a little or serve them immediately placed on top of the rocket. Pour over the dressing and toss to combine.

NB: For extra flavour, try adding some diced feta cheese.

Did you know? *Beetroot is a rich source of potassium. Studies have shown that potassium can help protect you from kidney stones.*

Beetroot and cumin colourful salad

The roasted beetroot and cumin combined with salads, fruit and vegetables make this salad divine. Every mouthful is an explosion of flavours and nutrients!

• Place the coconut oil in an ovenproof dish and melt on the high rack at 200°C for 2 minutes. Miss out this step if using olive oil.

• Place the onion and beetroots in the dish and toss well to coat in the oil. Sprinkle with the cumin seeds and return to the oven on the high rack for a further 20 minutes, turning regularly.

• Test for doneness: if the beetroot is not yet cooked, pop it back on the lower rack and cook until soft.

• Place the salad leaves in a large serving dish or individual dishes. Add all the remaining ingredients and combine with the cooked beetroot.

• When ready to serve, drizzle with the vinaigrette.

1–2 tsp coconut oil or olive oil

1 large red onion, peeled and cut into wedges

4 beetroots, peeled and cut into chunks

1–2 tsp cumin seeds

150g mixed peppery salad leaves

1 large carrot, peeled and grated

1 apple, diced

1 orange, peeled and diced

1 stick of celery, diced

$1/4$ cucumber, diced

8 cherry tomatoes, halved

2–3 tsp mixed seeds

2 tbsp low-fat vinaigrette

4

125g lean bacon
100g peppery salad leaves
$^1/_2$ bunch of spring onions, finely chopped
175g peas (fresh, or defrosted if frozen)
75g sugar snap peas, roughly chopped
Salad dressing
Salt and freshly ground black pepper

Bacon and pea salad

The natural saltiness and crispness of the bacon works so well with the mildness of the peas – I combine this with peppery salad leaves.

• Place the bacon on the grill rack (see p.3) and grill at 250°C for 4–5 minutes on each side, or until crispy.

• Meanwhile, place the salad leaves in a large serving bowl and mix in the spring onions, peas and sugar snap peas.

• Remove the bacon from the oven and roughly chop.

• Combine with the salad leaves and drizzle with a little salad dressing. Season to taste.

• Serve immediately.

Warm beetroot salad

I really love warm salads – they make a welcome change from steamed vegetables.

• Place the root vegetables (all cubed to a similar size) in a tin or browning tray.

• Drizzle with coconut oil or olive oil and toss to coat evenly. Sprinkle with the oregano, add a drizzle of balsamic vinegar and season.

• Place on the high rack and cook at 210°C for 20 minutes, or until soft and sweet.

• Meanwhile, toss the salad leaves with the red onion (or spring onion) and red pepper, and divide onto four serving dishes.

• When the vegetables are cooked, place in the centre of the salad leaves and top with a sprinkle of feta or goat's cheese.

• Serve immediately.

Did you know? *Beetroot is a great blood purifier. It is rich in bioflavonoids, carotenoids, vitamin C, folic acid and manganese.*

2–3 beetroots, peeled and cubed
2–3 parsnips, peeled and cubed
1–2 small sweet potatoes, peeled and cubed
Coconut oil or olive oil
1 tsp dried oregano
Balsamic vinegar
Salt and freshly ground black pepper
4 generous handfuls of seasonal salad leaves, washed
1 red onion, peeled and sliced (or spring onions, sliced)
1 red pepper, sliced
100g feta or soft goat's cheese

Roasted pecan, orange and feta salad

75g pecan nuts
125g peppery salad
   leaves
2–3 oranges,
   peeled and sliced
80g low-fat feta
   cheese, crumbled
Drizzle of low-fat
   vinaigrette

Place this salad on a bed of spinach, watercress and peppery lettuce leaves – it really needs that contrast. Fantastic on its own or as an accompaniment.

● Put the pecans on a baking tray and place on the high rack. Cook at 210°C for 5–8 minutes. Keep an eye on them as you don't want them to burn.

● Place the salad leaves in a large serving dish. Add the orange slices and feta cheese.

● Sprinkle with the pecans and drizzle with a little low-fat vinaigrette dressing.

● Serve immediately.

Did you know? *Feta is a good source of calcium and vitamins B2 and B12. It is high in fat, however, so opt for a low-fat version.*

Hot tomato and mozzarella salad

This is a simple salad with a big twist! Place plump cherry tomatoes roasted with garlic and thyme on a bed of peppery salad leaves and top with mozzarella chunks. Drizzle with balsamic vinegar or virgin olive oil for a really delicious salad.

• Pierce each tomato with the tip of a very sharp knife – this will stop them from exploding when cooking.

• Place the tomatoes on a baking tray or ovenproof dish. Scatter the garlic and thyme around the tomatoes.

• Drizzle with a little olive oil and sprinkle with a small amount of salt and sugar.

• Place on the high rack and cook at 200°C for 15 minutes.

• Meanwhile, place the salad leaves in a serving dish.

• When the tomatoes are cooked, place them with the garlic and thyme onto the salad leaves. Top with the mozzarella chunks.

• Finish with a drizzle of balsamic vinegar or extra-virgin olive oil.

• Serve immediately.

Did you know? *Tomatoes are a great source of carotenoid lycopene, which has been shown to help protect against cardiovascular disease.*

---

1 punnet of cherry or vine tomatoes, left whole
2 cloves of garlic, peeled and roughly chopped
2 sprigs of thyme
Drizzle of olive oil
Tiny sprinkle of low-sodium salt
Sprinkle of xylitol or sugar
125g peppery salad leaves
80g mozzarella, cut into chunks
Balsamic vinegar or extra-virgin olive oil

Goat's cheese and sun-dried tomato tower

2 portobello
    mushrooms (or
    large flat
    mushrooms)
Garlic-infused olive
    oil
100g goat's cheese
Freshly ground
    black pepper
2 generous
    handfuls of a
    selection of salad
    leaves (ideally
    rocket,
    watercress,
    spinach and
    lettuce leaves)
7.5–10cm piece of
    cucumber, diced
1/2 red pepper,
    diced
2–3 spring onions,
    chopped
1/2 green apple,
    diced
1/2 orange, peeled
    and sliced
8–10 cherry
    tomatoes, halved
25g toasted pine
    nuts or seeds
2 slices of ciabatta
    bread
4–6 sun-dried
    tomatoes in oil,
    drained
Drizzle of balsamic
    vinegar
Drizzle of sweet
    chilli sauce

Not so much a tower I suppose, but definitely an eye-catching and very, very tasty dish. This takes a maximum of 15 minutes to prepare and looks very professional – excellent for a quick and tasty supper, or reduce the quantities and serve as a dinner-party starter.

● Wash the mushrooms, remove the stalks and brush with the garlic-infused oil. Fill the mushrooms with goat's cheese and season with black pepper.

● Place the mushrooms on the high rack and cook at 220°C for 8 minutes.

● Meanwhile, place the salad leaves on two dinner plates. Sprinkle over the cucumber, red pepper, spring onions, apple, orange slices, cherry tomatoes and toasted pine nuts or seeds.

● When the halogen beeps, add the ciabatta slices to the high rack and cook for a further 3–4 minutes.

● When ready, place a ciabatta slice in the centre of each plate. Top with the stuffed mushroom and 2–3 sun-dried tomatoes.

● Finish with a drizzle of balsamic vinegar and sweet chilli sauce.

● Serve immediately.

Did you know? *Carotenoids are found in green vegetables such as spinach and broccoli, as well as rocket, sweetcorn and egg yolk.*

Rainbow coleslaw

I make a big batch of this and keep it in an airtight container in the fridge for up to two days, ready for when I want to add a dollop to a meal, sandwich or wrap.

- Place the cabbage in a large serving dish. Add the carrots and spring onions.

- Stir in the mayonnaise, mustard, lemon juice and zest.

- Place the coconut oil on a baking tray and melt on the high rack at 200°C for 1 minute.

- Toss the seeds in the oil and cook for 3–4 minutes.

- Stir into the coleslaw and serve.

$1/2$ head of red cabbage, shredded

3 carrots, peeled and grated

4 spring onions, finely sliced

2–3 tbsp low-fat mayonnaise

2 tsp wholegrain mustard

Juice and zest of 1 lemon

1 tsp coconut oil

3 tbsp mixed seeds

Did you know? *Carrots are packed with beta carotene, which our body converts to vitamin A. Vitamin A is known to help with eye health, and a lack of it is said to cause night blindness, which is why we are always told to eat plenty of carrots to see in the dark!*

Quinoa and roasted pumpkin seed salad

125g quinoa
6 cherry tomatoes, chopped
1 small red onion, peeled and finely chopped
1 red pepper, diced
1/4 cucumber, diced
1 stick of celery, finely diced
1 large carrot, peeled and grated
2–3 tbsp sweetcorn (tinned, or defrosted if frozen)
1 eating apple, skin on, cored and diced
80g pumpkin seeds
1 tbsp coconut oil or olive oil
Vinaigrette dressing

I love quinoa – it is so easy to cook and provides a good source of protein and fibre. Mix it with the vegetables and zinc-rich pumpkin seeds and you can see why this is such a great salad. Use a flax-oil vinaigrette dressing to add more Omega-3 to your meal.

• Place the quinoa in a saucepan with approximately 350ml of boiling water. Simmer gently until the quinoa has softened but still has bite – you don't want it to be mushy! If the water has not evaporated, drain off any excess and transfer the quinoa to a large serving dish.

• Toss in all the remaining ingredients, apart from the oil, pumpkin seeds and dressing.

• Place the pumpkin seeds in a small bowl and toss in the oil.

• Tip the seeds onto a baking tray, spreading them out so that the seeds are all lying flat.

• Place on the high rack (the grill rack preferably) and grill at 235°C for 1–3 minutes, turning the seeds until they are lightly toasted.

• Pour into the salad and toss well to combine.

• When ready to serve, drizzle over the vinaigrette dressing.

Did you know? *Pumpkin seeds are not only a good source of zinc but also magnesium – one of the most important and most used minerals in your body.*

Roasted chorizo, tomato and chickpea salad

I love the explosion of flavours in this salad. The chorizo oozes a rich paprika oil so there is no need to add a dressing. Serve with peppery salad leaves such as spinach, watercress and rocket.

• Place the chorizo in an ovenproof dish. (You do not need to add any oil as the chorizo will ooze oil as soon as it starts to heat up.)

• Place on the high rack and grill at 235°C for 3–5 minutes, until the chorizo starts to give up the oils and becomes golden.

• Pierce the tomatoes slightly using a sharp knife. Add the tomatoes, garlic, lemon zest and chickpeas to the chorizo, stir to combine and cook for a further 5 minutes.

• Meanwhile, place the salad leaves and onion in a serving dish.

• Add the chorizo mixture, toss to combine and serve immediately.

Did you know? *Spinach is rich in antioxidants, manganese, magnesium and beta carotene.*

2–3 chorizo sausages, sliced
8–12 cherry or vine tomatoes
2 cloves of garlic, peeled and roughly chopped
Zest of 1 lemon
400g can chickpeas, drained
2–3 large handfuls of peppery salad leaves
1 small red onion, peeled and finely sliced

Roasted potato, egg and ham salad

1 tsp coconut oil
1kg baby new
  potatoes
2–3 cloves of garlic,
  peeled and
  roughly chopped
2–3 sprigs of thyme
Freshly ground
  black pepper
2–3 eggs
2 handfuls of
  rocket, spinach
  and watercress
  leaves
1 red onion, peeled
  and sliced
8–12 cherry
  tomatoes, halved
4–6 slices of
  Wiltshire ham,
  roughly chopped
Light dressing or
  balsamic vinegar

This is an interesting variation on ham, egg and chips! If you don't want to use ham you could go for chicken or diced feta cheese instead.

• Place the coconut oil in an ovenproof dish and melt at 200°C for 2 minutes.

• Meanwhile, wash the potatoes. They need to be bite-size so if they're too big cut them in half. Ideally they should all be roughly the same size for an even cook.

• Remove the dish from the oven. Add the garlic, thyme and potatoes, tossing well in the oil. Season with a little black pepper.

• Place the dish on the high rack and roast for 30–45 minutes, turning occasionally until the potatoes are cooked.

• Meanwhile, hard-boil the eggs (6–7 minutes for softer hard-boiled eggs). Place immediately in cold water to cool before removing the shells and quartering.

• Place the salad leaves in a large bowl. Add the onion, cherry tomatoes and ham.

• Add the roasted new potatoes and eggs, and combine gently. Add a few splashes of light dressing or balsamic vinegar and season to taste.

• Serve immediately.

Meat

This chapter shows you some healthy ways to cook with meat. For those who really want to follow a healthy lifestyle, red meat should be limited to no more than two or three meals a week. If you are watching your weight, try to limit the amount of saturated fat by removing any visible fat, opting for lean cuts of meat and draining any excess fat or oil as you cook. Speak to your butcher about healthier options.

Healthy beefburgers

1 onion, peeled and
finely chopped
1 clove of garlic,
peeled and
crushed
400g lean minced
beef
1 tbsp home-
prepared
wholemeal
breadcrumbs
1 egg, beaten
Handful of freshly
chopped parsley
1 tsp wholegrain
mustard
Salt and freshly
ground black
pepper
Coconut oil or olive
oil
Salad leaves
4 wholemeal baps

If you fancy a burger, make it yourself for a healthier, low-fat version. These burgers are very simple to make, with just a few herbs and spices. If you want more of a punch, add some chopped chillies, a touch of curry powder or some cumin. If you want to add some hidden vegetables, add some grated carrot and finely chopped peppers. Opt for the leanest beef you can find and serve in a wholegrain seeded roll packed with tasty salad leaves.

• Put the onion and garlic in a large bowl. Add the beef and breadcrumbs, and mix thoroughly.

• Add the egg, parsley and mustard. Season to taste.

• Mix thoroughly and form into four firm but moist balls. Use the palm of your hands to flatten the balls into patties.

• Refrigerate until you are ready to use them, or freeze them in layers (separate the burgers with baking parchment to prevent them sticking together).

• When you are ready to cook the burgers, brush them lightly with coconut oil or olive oil.

• Place directly on the high rack and grill at 250°C for 5–8 minutes on each side until golden.

• Garnish with salad and serve with wholemeal baps.

Crustless quiche Lorraine

*Cut out the fat from a quiche Lorraine by making this
delicious quiche without the pastry case.*

• Preheat the halogen oven to 200°C or use the
preheat setting.

• In a bowl, mix the milk and eggs together thoroughly
before adding the mustard powder and cayenne
pepper. Add the cheese, onion and bacon or ham.
Season well before pouring into a greased 20cm round
flan dish.

• Bake on the low rack for 30 minutes until the quiche
is golden and the centre firm. If the top starts to get
too dark, cover with foil, making sure it is secured in
place.

• Serve with green salad and steamed new potatoes.

200ml milk

3 eggs

$1/2$ tsp mustard
  powder

Pinch of cayenne
  pepper

150g Gruyère
  cheese, grated

1 small onion,
  peeled and finely
  chopped

75g cooked ham or
  lean bacon, diced

Salt and freshly
  ground black
  pepper

Leek and cabbage roasted lamb chops

1/2 small savoy
    cabbage,
    shredded
1–2 leeks, sliced
2 tbsp butter or
    low-fat
    margarine,
    melted
1 tbsp wholegrain
    mustard
4 lamb chops
Mashed potatoes
    and mint sauce,
    to serve

I love creating layers with food for an explosion of flavours. Leek and cabbage are perfect together. Serve with mashed potato and a dollop of mint sauce.

• Place the cabbage and leeks in a greased deep roasting tin.

• Melt the butter and stir in the mustard. Pour over the cabbage and leeks and combine well.

• Place the lamb chops on top of the cabbage and leeks.

• Place on the low rack and cook at 200°C for 20 minutes, or until the chops are cooked to perfection (timings will vary depending on the size of the chops and how you like them cooked).

• Serve with mashed potato and mint sauce.

Did you know? *Dark green leafy vegetables are packed with magnesium. Other magnesium-rich foods include wholegrains, bean, pulses, nuts and seeds.*

Chilli con carne pie

Chilli and sweet potato are a match made in heaven. This is a lovely dish for all the family – you can make it as mild or hot as you like.

• In your sauté pan, add the coconut oil, followed by the onion, garlic, chilli, red pepper and celery. Cook until the vegetables start to soften.

• Add the mince and cook until it starts to brown. Drain away any excess fat before adding the spices, tomatoes, kidney beans, stock cube and chocolate. Add a little water if the mixture is looking too dry. Simmer on a very low heat for 10 minutes.

• Place the diced potatoes in a steamer and steam until soft.

• Mash with a little milk and season to taste.

• Place the mince mixture in a large ovenproof dish or small individual dishes, but don't overfill them. Spread the mash over the top and smooth down gently with a fork.

• Place on the low rack and cook for 15–20 minutes until golden and bubbling.

• Serve immediately.

Make ahead! This dish can be frozen, so plan ahead and fill your freezer with individual pies.

Healthy option! If you want to cut down on saturated fats, opt for minced turkey or Quorn.

---

1 tsp coconut oil
1 large onion, peeled and diced
2 cloves of garlic, peeled and finely chopped
1 chilli, finely chopped (deseeded if you don't want it too hot)
1 red pepper, finely diced
1 stick of celery, finely diced
400g extra-lean minced beef (or use lean minced turkey or Quorn)
$1/2$ tsp cumin
1 tsp chilli powder
1 tsp paprika
1 tsp marjoram
400g can chopped tomatoes
400g can red kidney beans, drained
$1/2$ low-salt beef stock cube (I use the jelly-type stock pots)
2 squares of dark chocolate (at least 70% cocoa)
600g sweet potatoes, peeled and diced
1 large white potato, peeled and diced
Dash of skimmed milk
Salt and freshly ground black

Coconut oil or olive
oil
2 x 200g lamb neck
fillets
4–6 sweet potatoes,
peeled
200g green beans
Butter
Salt and freshly
ground black
pepper

Seared lamb with sweet potato mash and green beans

A lovely dish for a dinner party or when you want to impress.

• Drizzle a little coconut oil or olive oil in a sauté pan. Sear the lamb fillets for 4–5 minutes, turning until browned all over.

• Transfer to a baking tray. Place on the high rack and cook at 180°C for 10–12 minutes, depending on the thickness of the meat and how you like it cooked.

• Meanwhile, place the sweet potatoes in a pan of boiling water or steam until soft.

• Remove the lamb from the oven, wrap it in foil and leave to rest.

• Place the green beans in the steamer or boil for 5–8 minutes.

• Mash the sweet potato with a knob of butter and season to taste.

• Place the lamb on a bed of mash and serve with the green beans.

Skinny moussaka

A taste of Greece! You can prepare this in advance and it is also suitable for freezing.

• Place the aubergines in a pan of boiling water for 2 minutes. Remove and pat dry. Leave to one side.

• Meanwhile, heat the oil in a sauté pan and fry the onion and garlic. Add the lamb and cook until brown.

• Add the tomatoes, tomato purée, mint, cinnamon and seasoning, and cook for a further 2–3 minutes.

• Select an ovenproof dish – I normally use a Pyrex or lasagne dish. Preheat the halogen oven to 210°C or use the preheat setting.

• Place a layer of mince in the dish, followed by a layer of aubergine slices. Alternate the mince and aubergine layers, finishing with a layer of mince.

• In a bowl, mix the quark and Greek yoghurt with half the cheese (if it is too thick add a little skimmed milk – it should be the consistency of custard). Season to taste with black pepper and pour over the top. Sprinkle with the remaining cheese.

• Place on the low rack and cook for 20–25 minutes until bubbling.

Healthy tip! You can make this dish healthier by using lean minced turkey or Quorn.

2–3 aubergines, sliced
1 tsp coconut oil or olive oil
1 red onion, peeled and finely diced
2 cloves of garlic, peeled and crushed
400g extra-lean minced lamb
400g can chopped tomatoes
2 tsp tomato purée
1 tsp dried mint
2 tsp ground cinnamon
Salt and freshly ground black pepper
150g quark
150g Greek yoghurt
50g mature Cheddar or Parmesan cheese, grated
50ml skimmed milk (if needed)

60ml olive oil

¹/₂ bunch of spring onions, chopped

Juice and rind of 2 lemons

2.5cm piece of fresh ginger, peeled and finely chopped

2 cloves of garlic, peeled and crushed

Small handful of fresh coriander, finely chopped

200ml Greek yoghurt (I use Total as it holds while cooking)

Salt and freshly ground black pepper

4 pork chops

Coriander leaves, to garnish

Lemon and ginger pork chops

You will need to marinate these chops, ideally for about 4 hours, to get lovely, moist and flavoursome chops. Once marinated, simply pop in the oven and cook for 20 minutes – so easy!

• In a bowl, mix all the ingredients together, apart from the chops. Once combined, add the chops, ensuring they are fully covered in the marinade. (You can do this in the bowl you made the marinade in, or place the marinade in a freezer bag, add the chops and shake well to cover.)

• Place the marinating chops in the fridge for at least 4 hours.

• When ready to cook, place the chops in an oiled ovenproof dish and cover with the marinade.

• Preheat the halogen oven to 190°C.

• Place on the high rack and cook for 20 minutes, or until the chops are cooked to your liking.

• Garnish with coriander leaves.

Did you know? *Ginger is great for cleansing the body, but also helps settle the stomach, particularly if you suffer from nausea.*

Lamb biryani

You can prepare this dish in advance so it is perfect for a dinner party or when you want a relaxing evening without slaving over the cooker.

• Heat the oil in a sauté pan. Add the lamb, onion and garlic, and cook until the lamb starts to brown and the onion starts to soften.

• Add the spices and cook for a couple of minutes before adding the yoghurt and tomatoes. Combine well and cook on a low heat for 10 minutes.

• Meanwhile, cook the rice according to packet instructions. I usually add $1^1/2$ cups of water to each cup of rice. Bring to the boil and simmer for a couple of minutes before covering and removing from the heat. Leave to stand for 10–12 minutes, then fluff up using a fork.

• When the rice is done, place a layer in the bottom of an ovenproof dish. Follow this with a layer of the lamb mixture. Continue until you have used up all the ingredients, then cover with foil.

• Place on the high rack and cook at 180°C for 20 minutes.

• Garnish with the toasted almonds before serving.

Coconut oil or olive oil
600g lamb, cubed
1 onion, peeled and diced
3 cloves of garlic, peeled and crushed
1 tsp ground cinnamon
1 tsp ground cardamom
1 tsp ground cloves
1 tbsp curry powder
300ml fat-free Greek yoghurt
3 tomatoes, diced
250g long-grain rice
Sprinkle of toasted almonds, to garnish

Did you know? *Onions are not only packed with quercetin, they are also a good source of chromium, which can help maintain a positive hormone balance, decrease cholesterol and prevent those annoying mid-afternoon energy slumps!*

Serves

4

2 red onions,
  peeled and cut
  into wedges
2 courgettes,
  thickly sliced
2 red peppers,
  thickly sliced
$1/2$ aubergine,
  thickly sliced
2 sweet potatoes,
  skins on and
  sliced
12 cherry tomatoes
$1/2$ bulb of garlic,
  whole and
  unpeeled
3 sprigs of rosemary
Coconut oil or olive
  oil
Salt and freshly
  ground black
  pepper
Sugar
Balsamic vinegar
Handful of black or
  green olives
4 lamb steaks
Garlic-infused olive
  oil

Lamb steaks with Mediterranean vegetables

The halogen oven makes the most delicious roasted vegetables, which work perfectly with lamb steaks.

• Add all the vegetables to a large ovenproof dish, combining well (the garlic skins will be removed later). Place the rosemary in amongst the vegetables.

• Drizzle with oil, a sprinkle of salt, a tiny sprinkle of sugar and a small drizzle of balsamic vinegar (not too much or you will overpower the dish).

• Place on the high rack and cook at 190°C for 30 minutes, then add the olives and a little more oil if needed. Return to the oven for another 10 minutes.

• Brush the lamb steaks with a little garlic oil and season to taste.

• Remove the vegetables and place them in the base of the halogen oven.

• Turn the temperature up to 250°C and place the steaks on the grill rack. Grill for 5–8 minutes on each side (this depends on how close the steaks are to the heat and also on how you like your meat done, so test every few minutes).

• To serve, place the steaks on each plate and spoon over the vegetables.

Did you know? Research by the University of Bern in Switzerland found that onions contain GPCS peptide, which is said to inhibit loss of bone minerals and calcium, making onions effective against osteoporosis.

Wholegrain mustard steak salad

I pinched this recipe from my mum. It is one of her favourites as she loves wholegrain mustard. Hope you enjoy it too!

- Place the steaks on the grill rack (see p.3).

- Grill on one side for approximately 4–5 minutes.

- Turn over and spread the top of the steaks with wholegrain mustard. Grill for a further 4–5 minutes (cooking times will vary depending on the height of the rack and the thickness of the steaks – adjust to suit your own requirements).

- Remove from the oven and wrap the steaks in foil. Leave to rest while you prepare the salad.

- Put the salad leaves, onion and cherry tomatoes in a serving dish.

- In a small jar make the dressing by mixing the oil and vinegar and season to taste.

- Toss the salad leaves with the dressing.

- Unwrap the steaks and cut into thick slices. Place the slices on top of the salad, toss and serve immediately.

2–3 fillet steaks
3 tbsp wholegrain mustard
1 bag of peppery mixed leaf salad
1 red onion, peeled and finely sliced
12–16 cherry tomatoes, halved
2 tbsp olive oil
1–2 tbsp white wine vinegar
Salt and freshly ground black pepper

Pork, vegetable and bean casserole

1 tsp coconut oil or
olive oil
400g lean pork, cut
into chunks
1 large onion,
peeled and diced
1 large red or green
pepper, diced
2 cloves of garlic,
peeled and
crushed
2 sticks of celery,
diced
2 carrots, peeled
and diced
1–2 sweet potatoes,
peeled and diced
2 eating apples,
skins on, cored
and chopped
400g can chopped
tomatoes
400g can cannellini
beans, drained
2 tsp sun-dried
tomato purée
600ml chicken
stock
1 tsp chopped
parsley
2 tsp paprika
Freshly ground
black pepper

I urge everyone to start adding beans or pulses to dishes – casseroles especially. It raises the nutrient quality and adds essential fibre, helping to keep you fuller for longer. Ideal for those on a budget as it is an economical way to add protein and fibre and helps bulk out a meal. This dish is suitable for freezing.

• Heat the oil in a sauté pan and add the pork. Brown gently then transfer to an ovenproof casserole dish.

• Add the onion, red or green pepper, garlic, celery, carrots and sweet potatoes to the pan and cook for 5 minutes to soften.

• Add this to the casserole dish along with the remaining ingredients. Season with black pepper.

• Place on the low rack with a double layer of foil as a lid and cook at 160°C for 2 hours.

• Serve immediately.

Did you know? *Beans are rich in folic acid and B vitamins.*

Spiced pork steaks

You will need to marinate these pork steaks for at least 6 hours before grilling. They can be prepared the night before or in the morning before leaving for work. The steaks really do benefit from this marinating time.

• Place the pork steaks on a chopping board and use a rolling pin or meat mallet to flatten them. Place the pork in a plastic food bag.

• Place the remaining ingredients in a bowl and combine well.

• Tip the yoghurt mixture into the bag with the pork and shake to coat the steaks.

• Refrigerate for at least 6 hours or overnight.

• Bring out to room temperature for at least 1 hour before cooking.

• Place a foil-lined baking tray on the high rack. Place the low rack over this to create a grill rack – the baking tray below will collect any mess from the pork. If you don't have a grill rack, then improvise to get as near to the element as you can without touching it!

• Place the steaks on the grill rack and grill on both sides at 235°C for 5–10 minutes until done. Brush on any additional marinade as you grill if you wish.

• Serve with boiled new potatoes and salad.

Did you know? *Chillies contain capsaicin, which has been shown to help reduce the appetite as well as speed up the metabolism.*

---

4 lean pork steaks
$^1/_2$ tsp cayenne pepper
$^1/_2$ tsp chilli powder
$^1/_2$ tsp turmeric
2 tsp paprika
$^1/_2$ tsp ground cumin
$^1/_2$–1 chilli, finely chopped (deseeded if you don't want it too hot)
2 cloves of garlic, peeled and finely chopped
2cm piece of ginger, peeled and finely grated
3 tbsp fat-free Greek yoghurt
Juice and zest of 1 lemon
Boiled new potatoes and salad, to serve

Moroccan-style kebabs

2 tsp paprika
1 tsp cumin
1 tsp turmeric
2 tsp ground
    cinnamon
1 tsp allspice
1 tsp ground
    cardamom
2 tsp ground ginger
Freshly ground
    black pepper
Small handful of
    fresh coriander
2 chillies (deseeded
    if you don't want
    it too hot)
2 cloves of garlic,
    peeled
2 tbsp olive oil, plus
    extra for drizzling
400g lamb loin,
    diced
2–3 red onions,
    peeled and cut
    into wedges
12–16 dried
    apricots
Savoury rice or
    couscous, to
    serve

Kebabs can be made in advance – these certainly benefit from marinating for several hours before cooking. I have used dried apricots and red onions but you can add whatever you fancy.

• Place all the spices and coriander in a food processor along with the chillies, garlic and oil, and whiz to form a paste.

• Place the diced lamb in a plastic food bag and pour in the spiced paste. Secure and refrigerate overnight. If you are using wooden skewers, soak them in water.

• When ready to prepare, remove the lamb from the fridge and bring up to room temperature.

• Place the onion wedges in an ovenproof dish and drizzle with a little oil.

• Place on the high rack and cook at 210°C for 10 minutes to soften.

• Thread the lamb, apricots and onion onto 8 skewers. Keep any leftover paste to brush over the lamb as it cooks.

• Place the skewers on the high rack (or grill rack if you have one). Increase the temperature to 235°C or high and grill, turning and basting regularly, for 10–15 minutes until the lamb is cooked.

• Serve on a bed of savoury rice or couscous.

Did you know? *Chillies contain capsaicin, which helps raise your body temperature, increasing your metabolism and allowing you to burn more calories.*

Garlic and chilli lamb chops

Serves
4

Lamb chops can be a bit dull, so liven them up with some chilli and garlic.

- Remove any fat from the lamb chops.

- In a blender, whiz the chillies, garlic, lime zest and oil. Season to taste.

- Pour over the lamb chops and marinate for 2 hours in the fridge.

- When ready to cook, place on a browning tray. Place the tray on the high rack and cook at 250°C for 6–8 minutes on both sides until the chops are cooked.

- Serve with boiled new potatoes and green vegetables.

Did you know? *Garlic is great for boosting the immune system.*

---

8 lamb chops
2–3 chillies
4 cloves of garlic, peeled
Zest of $1/2$ lime
2 tbsp olive oil
Salt and freshly ground black pepper
Boiled new potatoes and green vegetables, to serve

Poultry

Chicken is a good source of protein, niacin and selenium. It also contains vitamin B6 and phosphorus. Dark chicken meat contains more zinc and B vitamins than white chicken meat but it also contains much more fat, so if you are watching your weight you are better off sticking with the leaner white chicken meat. Remember to remove all visible fat and skin as this really does pile on the calories.

Turkey is rich in protein and selenium but is roughly two-thirds lower in fat than chicken – but remember much depends on how you cook it! Turkey contains carnosine, which has been shown to help slow down ageing. As with chicken, the darker meat is higher in fat, so avoid this if you are watching your weight.

I prefer to buy free-range or organic meat. Many supermarkets are now offering this at much cheaper prices and you will be surprised how much nicer it tastes.

Remember the rules when handling raw chicken: always clean utensils and chopping boards thoroughly after use to avoid the spread of bacteria. Never cook chicken from frozen; always make sure it is thoroughly defrosted, ideally in the fridge. Finally, always make sure chicken is cooked through.

Griddled chicken with baked tomatoes and spinach

1 punnet of cherry
tomatoes
3–4 cloves of garlic,
peeled and
roughly chopped
2 sprigs of thyme
Olive oil
Balsamic vinegar
Salt and freshly
ground black
pepper
1 tsp xylitol or
brown sugar
4 skinless chicken
fillets, fat
removed
100g baby leaf
spinach, washed
1 red onion, peeled
and finely
chopped

This is one of my favourite recipes – I love the flavours of baked tomatoes, garlic and balsamic vinegar. You can, of course, grill the chicken in the halogen if you prefer (place it on the high rack at the highest temperature and grill on both sides until cooked), but I love the look of griddled chicken.

• Place the tomatoes on a baking tray, and add the garlic and thyme, making sure some of it covers the tomatoes. Drizzle with oil and balsamic vinegar.

• Season and add the xylitol or brown sugar.

• Place on the low rack and bake at 190°C for 20 minutes.

• Meanwhile, griddle the chicken. Cook on both sides until browned and cooked thoroughly.

• Remove the tomatoes from the oven. Place the spinach in a bowl with the onion. Pour over the tomatoes and gently toss to combine.

• Divide the spinach and tomato mixture between four plates and place the chicken on top.

• Drizzle with a little oil and balsamic vinegar to taste. Season to taste before serving.

Did you know? *Spinach is a rich source of the B vitamin folic acid – vital for women who are planning to conceive or are pregnant. Other sources of folate include broccoli, lentils, avocado and asparagus.*

Easy Cajun chicken with roasted sweet potatoes

Serves

4

If you like spicy food you'll love this Cajun chicken dish. You can add some chopped chillies if you like a really hot dish, but personally, I think this is spicy enough!

- Preheat the halogen oven to 200°C. Melt the coconut oil in an ovenproof dish in the halogen for 1–2 minutes.

- Place the sweet potatoes and onions in the ovenproof dish. Toss in the oil to coat. Sprinkle with paprika and season to taste.

- Place on the high rack and cook at 200°C for 10 minutes.

- Meanwhile, score the chicken using a sharp knife. In a small bowl, combine the Cajun spice with the agave syrup, lime juice and zest.

- Using a pastry brush, coat the chicken breasts with the Cajun mixture, making sure you press it into the cuts.

- Remove the tray from the oven and add the chicken breasts to the potato and onion wedges. If you have any Cajun mixture left, use it to coat the potatoes.

- Return to the high rack and cook for a further 15–20 minutes, or until the chicken is thoroughly cooked.

- Serve with a green salad.

2–3 tsp coconut oil
6 sweet potatoes, skins on, cut into thick wedges
2 red onions, peeled and cut into wedges
Paprika
Salt and freshly ground black pepper
4–6 skinless chicken pieces
2–3 tbsp Cajun spice
2 tbsp agave syrup
Juice and zest of 1 lime
Green salad, to serve

Healthy swap! *Reduce the saturated fat of the dish by swapping chicken for turkey.*

Did you know? *Onions are an excellent natural source of prebiotics, stimulating the growth and function of certain 'good' bacteria in the gut and helping to support natural defences.*

Tuscan-style chicken

1 large red onion,
  peeled and cut
  into wedges
3–4 cloves of garlic,
  peeled and
  roughly chopped
1 red pepper,
  thickly sliced
100g pancetta or
  lean bacon,
  thickly diced
4 skinless chicken
  breasts
1 punnet of cherry
  tomatoes
Olive oil
Balsamic vinegar
Salt and freshly
  ground black
  pepper
Paprika
2–3 sprigs of thyme
75g green or black
  olives (optional)
400g can chopped
  tomatoes
Handful of basil
  leaves
400g can borlotti
  beans, drained
400g can haricot
  beans, drained
100ml hot chicken
  stock or red wine

This dish started out as a basic one-pot tomato, garlic and basil with chicken but my son decided he wanted to bulk it out (he is a very hungry university student!), so added beans, chopped tomatoes and peppers – the result was delicious and wholesome.

• Put the onion, garlic, red pepper, pancetta or bacon, chicken and cherry tomatoes in a large baking tray. Make sure they are evenly distributed.

• Drizzle with olive oil and a little balsamic vinegar.

• Season to taste and add a little paprika. Place the thyme sprigs next to the chicken.

• Place on the high rack and bake at 200°C for 15–20 minutes, turning the chicken halfway through cooking. Remove from the oven and add the olives, tomatoes, basil leaves and beans. Add the stock, or if you are feeling daring, red wine, and gently combine.

• Return to the oven for a further 10 minutes.

• Serve immediately.

Cooking tip! *If you have a small halogen oven you may want to split this dish onto two trays and cook on the high and low racks, swapping halfway through cooking. If you don't have a baking tray with deep sides, use a casserole dish instead.*

Healthy turkey burgers

There is no reason why you can't have a burger when following a healthy diet; however, it is best to grill rather than fry the burger. This recipe uses turkey, which is lower in saturated fat than chicken and much lower than red meat.

• Place all the ingredients in a bowl and mix thoroughly.

• Form into four balls – these should be firm but moist. If the mixture is dry, add a little beaten egg.

• Use the palm of your hands to flatten the balls into patties.

• Refrigerate until you are ready to use them, or freeze them in layers (separate the burgers with baking parchment to prevent them sticking together).

• When you are ready to cook the burgers, spray a baking tray with a little olive oil. Put the burgers on the tray and place on the high rack.

• Set the temperature to 250°C and grill on both sides for 8–10 minutes until cooked. Be careful when turning these over as they are quite fragile. Wait until the meat is white on one side before turning.

• Serve with wholemeal baps, a salad garnish and a dollop of fat-free mayonnaise or a drizzle of sweet chilli sauce.

Did you know? *Lean turkey is a good source of protein, but also carnosine, which some research suggests could help slow down the ageing process.*

---

1 red onion, peeled and finely chopped
2 cloves of garlic, peeled and crushed
1 stick of celery, chopped
½ yellow pepper, chopped
300g minced turkey
30g pine nuts, crushed
1 tsp curry powder
1 tbsp home-prepared wholemeal breadcrumbs
Freshly ground black pepper
Beaten egg (if needed)
Olive oil
Wholemeal baps, salad, fat-free mayonnaise or sweet chilli sauce, to serve

Chilli-stuffed chicken

2–4 tbsp quark or
   fat-free Greek
   yoghurt
1–2 red chillies,
   finely chopped
$1/2$ tsp chilli powder
Salt and freshly
   ground black
   pepper
4 lean skinless
   chicken breasts
   (use turkey
   breasts if you
   prefer)
Coconut oil
Boiled brown and
   wild rice, and a
   green salad, to
   serve

A very simple dish that takes minutes to prepare.

• Place the quark or Greek yoghurt in a bowl and stir
in the chillies and chilli powder until combined.
Season to taste.

• Using a sharp knife, cut a slit in each chicken breast
to form a pocket. Stuff the pockets with the creamed
mixture.

• Grease an ovenproof dish with coconut oil. Place the
chicken breasts on top and season.

• Place on the high rack and cook at 190°C for 20–30
minutes until the chicken is cooked.

• Serve with brown and wild rice and a green salad.

Did you know? *Chicken is low in fat (compared to red
meat), rich in vitamins B3 and B6, selenium and
phosphorus.*

Cajun chicken with spicy salsa

This is a great quick-and-easy meal which you can prepare in advance. Leave the chicken to marinate for an hour or two to enhance the flavour.

• Cut the chicken breasts in half horizontally. Use a rolling pin or meat mallet to flatten the chicken until thin.

• Mix the spices together in a small bowl. Spray the chicken with oil before rubbing in the spice mixture. Set aside for at least 20 minutes.

• To make the salsa, mix the vegetables with the coriander and chilli. Stir in the lime juice and zest, oil and balsamic vinegar. Add more to taste if needed.

• Place the chicken on a foil-lined tray. Place on the high rack (or grill rack if you have one) and cook at 250°C for 5–6 minutes on each side until done. Serve on a bed of salsa.

4 skinless chicken breasts
2 tsp ground cumin
2 tsp ground coriander
2 tsp chilli powder
2 tsp paprika
Olive oil

For the salsa
$^1/_2$ cucumber, diced
1 red onion, peeled and diced
4–6 spring onions, including green stalks, sliced
1 red pepper, diced
1 yellow pepper, diced
10 cherry tomatoes, halved
Small handful of fresh coriander, chopped
1 chilli, finely diced
Juice and zest of $^1/_2$ lime
2 tbsp olive oil
2 tsp balsamic vinegar

Sticky sweet sugar-free chicken drumsticks

3 tbsp agave or
  Sweet Freedom
  syrup
1 tbsp mustard
1 tbsp
  Worcestershire
  sauce
1 tbsp soy sauce
2 tsp paprika
4 chicken
  drumsticks
Couscous and salad,
  to serve

These really are sticky and very, very tasty! The agave or Sweet Freedom syrup gives you the sweetness without raising your blood-sugar levels.

• Place all the ingredients, apart from the chicken, in a bowl and mix well.

• Score the chicken drumsticks using a sharp knife.

• Have a large plastic food bag ready – this can get messy! Place the drumsticks and the marinade in the bag. Shake well to ensure the drumsticks are thoroughly coated. Secure and leave in the fridge overnight.

• When you are ready to cook, as a precaution, line the baking tray with foil and place under the high rack to collect any mess.

• Place the drumsticks directly on the high rack. The advantage of cooking straight on the rack is that the meat cooks on all sides.

• Cook at 230°C for 15–20 minutes, turning and basting with the marinade as you go, if you like. Make sure the chicken is cooked through.

• Serve with couscous and salad.

Arrabiata chicken bake

This can be prepared in advance and left in the fridge until you are ready to cook. If you prefer a lower-fat version, opt for turkey fillets instead.

• Heat the oil on a medium heat in a sauté pan. Add the onion, red peppers, chilli, garlic and chicken, and cook until the chicken turns white on all sides.

• Add the chopped tomatoes, herbs and 3 tablespoons of water, and cook for a further 10 minutes.

• Meanwhile, mix the milk, crème fraîche and Cheddar together in a bowl. Season with black pepper.

• Divide the chicken mixture between the tortillas and roll – this can be messy! Place the rolled-up tortillas in an ovenproof dish and pour over the crème fraîche mixture. Add the tomato halves.

• Place on the low rack and cook at 180°C for 20 minutes until golden and bubbling. Serve immediately.

Did you know? *Diet-related diseases are two of the top five causes of premature death for people under 60 years old.*

Chilli oil

1 onion, peeled and sliced

2 red peppers, sliced

1 red chilli, finely sliced

2–3 cloves of garlic, peeled and roughly chopped

3–4 chicken fillets, diced

400g can chopped tomatoes

Small handful of chopped parsley

Few sprigs of chopped fresh thyme and oregano

200ml milk

300g crème fraîche

30g mature Cheddar cheese, grated

Freshly ground black pepper

8 wholemeal tortillas

4–6 cherry tomatoes, halved

Spicy chicken wings

1–2 chillies, finely chopped

2 cloves of garlic, peeled and finely chopped

2–3 tsp chilli sauce (mild or hot, depending on taste)

Juice and zest of 1 lemon

1 tsp paprika

1 tsp allspice

$^1/_2$ tsp ground ginger

$^1/_2$ tsp chilli powder

1 tbsp brown sugar or xylitol

2–3 tsp agave syrup

Salt and freshly ground black pepper

10–12 chicken wings

Boiled brown rice and salad, to serve

A really simple dish that takes minutes to prepare. Marinate overnight or for at least 1 hour before cooking. Serve with rice and salad for a great summer evening alfresco supper.

● In a bowl, combine all the ingredients, apart from the chicken wings. Add the chicken wings and coat in the marinade. Cover with clingfilm and leave to marinate in the fridge overnight or for at least 1 hour. If you don't have a big enough bowl, put the chicken wings and marinade in a large plastic food bag and shake to coat.

● Preheat the halogen oven to 210°C or use the preheat setting.

● Tip the wings and the coating into an ovenproof dish (or browning tray if you have one). Cook on the high rack for 20 minutes, or until the chicken is cooked through.

● Serve with brown rice and salad.

Healthy swap! *This dish is usually made with honey or maple syrup. Using agave syrup instead helps keep blood sugars stable.*

Chicken, bean and tomato one-pot

A tasty and filling one-pot.

• Preheat the halogen oven to 200°C or use the preheat setting.

• Spray a roasting tin or casserole dish with olive oil or melt a little coconut oil before adding the onions, red pepper, garlic, chicken and tomatoes. Spray with a little more oil, ensuring all the ingredients are coated in oil. Add the thyme and sprinkle with paprika.

• Place on the low rack and cook for 15 minutes. Remove from the oven and add the remaining ingredients. Combine well.

• Return to the oven and cook for a further 20 minutes until the chicken is cooked to perfection.

Healthy swap! *Swapping chicken for turkey fillets helps lower the fat content of this dish.*

Did you know? *I use red onions in most of my recipes as they contain great nutrients like quercetin; more so than regular onions. It has been suggested that red onions have cancer-fighting properties (as have green tea, turmeric, garlic and broccoli). Red onions also contain allicin, which helps fight disease and can help lower blood pressure.*

1–2 tsp coconut oil or olive oil

2 red onions, peeled and cut into small wedges

1 red pepper, sliced

3–4 cloves of garlic, peeled and finely chopped

4 chicken breasts, halved

1 small punnet of cherry tomatoes, left whole

Handful of fresh thyme (or 1–2 tsp dried thyme)

2 tsp paprika

450ml hot chicken stock

2–3 tsp sun-dried tomato purée

400g can cannellini beans, drained

Salt and freshly ground black pepper

Small handful of fresh parsley, finely chopped

Italian chicken pot roast

2 red onions,
    peeled and cut
    into wedges
2 red peppers, cut
    into wedges
2 courgettes, cut
    into thick slices
1/2 aubergine, cut
    into thick slices
2 sweet potatoes,
    skins on, cut into
    thick slices
12–16 cherry
    tomatoes, left
    whole
8–10 green or black
    olives (optional)
1 tbsp olive oil or
    coconut oil
1 tbsp balsamic
    vinegar
Freshly ground
    black pepper
4 chicken breasts
Paprika
3–4 rosemary or
    thyme sprigs

A really simple yet delicious pot roast – perfect for when you want a great meal with little effort.

• Place the vegetables in a bowl and add the olive oil or use melted coconut oil. Add the balsamic vinegar. Mix well with your hands, ensuring the vegetables are evenly coated.

• Tip the vegetables into a roasting tin and season with black pepper.

• Rub the chicken breasts with olive oil or coconut oil. Place them in the roasting tin, either on top of, or nestled in amongst, the vegetables.

• Sprinkle the chicken breasts with paprika; this adds flavour but also helps give a nice golden colour.

• Place the herbs in amongst the chicken and vegetables.

• Place on the low rack and roast at 200°C for 15 minutes. Remove and turn the chicken, adding more paprika if needed.

• Return to the oven and cook for a further 15–20 minutes, or until the chicken is cooked through.

Healthy swap! *Use turkey breasts for a lower-fat option, cut into small pieces. Remember to remove the skin and any visible fat. Use coconut oil instead of olive oil. Add the coconut oil to the roasting tin and place in the oven for 1 minute to melt before adding the vegetables.*

Low-fat tandoori chicken

This is a low-fat version of a favourite takeaway. There is something deeply satisfying about using herbs and spices when cooking, and it is a great way to get the family's attention as the flavours start to waft through the house.

• In a food processor, mix the garlic and spices with the lemon juice and zest, olive oil and yoghurt.

• Pour into a bowl, and stir in the chicken pieces. For the best flavour, leave to marinate for a few hours in the fridge.

• Preheat the halogen oven to 200°C or use the preheat setting.

• Place the chicken, marinade and onion in an ovenproof dish. Place on the low rack and cook for 35 minutes.

• Serve on a bed of rice.

Did you know? *Garlic is known for its detoxifying properties.*

2–3 cloves of garlic, crushed

1 tsp coriander powder

1 tsp cayenne pepper

1 tsp chilli powder (or fresh chillies, finely chopped)

1 tsp curry powder

2 tsp turmeric

2–3 tsp paprika

2.5cm piece of ginger, peeled and grated

Juice and zest of 1 lemon

Dash of olive oil

100g fat-free Greek yoghurt

4 large skinless pieces of chicken (thigh or breast)

1 onion, peeled and finely chopped

Basmati or brown rice, to serve

Stuffed red pesto and sun-dried tomato chicken

4 skinless chicken
breasts
4 heaped tsp red
pesto
3 tbsp quark or fat-
free Greek
yoghurt
8–12 sun-dried
tomatoes
(drained of oil),
chopped
Freshly ground
black pepper
Coconut oil
Boiled new
potatoes and
salad, to serve

You can use turkey instead of chicken if you prefer.

• Wash and dry the chicken, and cut a pocket in each breast.

• In a bowl, mix the pesto, quark or yoghurt and sun-dried tomatoes. Season with black pepper.

• Stuff the pockets with the paste, but do not overfill them or the paste will ooze out during cooking. Seal the pockets using a cocktail stick.

• Place on a baking tray greased with coconut oil.

• Place on the high rack and cook at 190°C for 20–30 minutes until the chicken is cooked through.

• Serve with boiled new potatoes and a green salad.

Healthy tip! Boost the Omega-3 in your diet by adding mixed seeds to salads. Inject a splash of colour to a green salad by adding grated carrot, beetroot, chopped peppers, apple and celery. Make a healthy omega-rich dressing using flax oil instead of olive oil.

Chilli chicken skewers with roasted vegetable salad

Serves

4

This is a really simple dish and can be made in advance as the chicken does benefit from being left to marinate.

- Place the chillies, garlic, oil and balsamic vinegar in a food processor and whiz until blended. Season with black pepper.

- Cut the chicken or turkey into chunks and place in a bowl. Pour two-thirds of the chilli mixture over the chicken and leave to marinate for at least 1 hour. Reserve the remaining marinade to use as a dressing later.

- Place the onions, tomatoes, peppers, courgettes and sweet potato in an ovenproof dish. Drizzle with a little olive oil.

- Place on the high rack and cook at 190°C for 15 minutes.

- Meanwhile, thread the chicken onto four skewers and brush with its marinade.

- Place the vegetables in the base of the halogen to keep warm.

- Place the skewers on the high rack (or grill rack if you have one). Turn the temperature up to 235°C and grill for about 10 minutes, turning the chicken regularly to stop it from burning and to ensure an even cook.

- Meanwhile, place the rocket in a large serving dish.

- When ready to serve, remove the vegetables from the oven and tip them over the rocket, tossing gently.

- Place the chicken skewers over the vegetables and drizzle with the reserved marinade dressing. Serve immediately.

2 chillies
3 cloves of garlic, peeled
4 tbsp olive oil, plus extra for drizzling
2 tbsp balsamic vinegar
Freshly ground black pepper
300g chicken or turkey fillet
2 red onions, peeled and sliced
8 tomatoes, halved
2 green, yellow, red or orange peppers
2 courgettes, thickly sliced
2 sweet potatoes, peeled and thickly sliced
75g rocket

Health swap! *Swapping chicken for turkey will reduce the amount of saturated fat in the dish.*

7

Chicken korma

1 tsp coconut oil

400g lean skinless chicken or turkey, diced

1 large onion, peeled and diced

2–3 cloves of garlic, peeled and roughly chopped

2.5cm piece of ginger, peeled and roughly chopped

$^1/_2$ tsp ground cinnamon

6 cardamom pods

3 cloves

$^1/_2$ tsp caraway seeds

$^1/_2$ tsp turmeric

2 tsp mild/medium curry powder

40g ground almonds

250ml hot chicken stock

150g fat-free Greek yoghurt

150ml low-fat coconut milk

30g desiccated coconut

Small handful of fresh coriander, chopped

Boiled basmati rice, to serve

You can use either chicken or turkey in this recipe. Most of this dish is cooked in a saucepan but you can use the halogen oven to cook the sauce. If you're short of time, make ahead and reheat.

• Put the coconut oil in a deep casserole or ovenproof dish. Place on the low rack and melt for 1 minute at 200°C.

• Add the chicken, onion, garlic and ginger. Cook for 5–8 minutes, turning occasionally. NB: If you prefer, you can do this in a sauté pan on the hob.

• In a pestle and mortar, grind the cinnamon, cardamom pods, cloves, caraway seeds, turmeric and curry powder. Mix this with the ground almonds before adding to the chicken. Stir well and then add the chicken stock. Cook for a further 10 minutes to bring up to temperature and then simmer, stirring occasionally.

• Stir in the yoghurt and coconut milk. Place a foil lid on the dish and cook for a further 15 minutes.

• Sprinkle with desiccated coconut and fresh coriander.

• Serve with basmati rice.

Did you know? *Basmati rice is low GI.*

Chilli and lemongrass chicken kebabs

This is a great simple supper if you want to plan ahead and enjoy some free time away from the kitchen. Soak the skewers (if using wooden ones) overnight or for a few hours while the chicken is marinating. Serve with fluffy rice and salad.

• If you have a food processor or mini processor, this will make your life so much easier. Simply add all the ingredients, apart from the chicken, and whiz to form a paste. If you don't have a processor, finely chop the ingredients (or use a pestle and mortar), add the oil and lime juice, and combine well.

• Place the mixture in a bowl or plastic food bag. Add the chicken chunks and marinate overnight or for 3–4 hours. At the same time, soak the skewers as this prevents them from burning.

• When ready to prepare, thread the chicken onto skewers. (You could add a cherry tomato or wedge of red pepper between each chicken chunk if you like.)

• Place the kebabs on the high rack (or grill rack if you have one) and grill at 250°C for no more than 10 minutes, turning regularly to make sure the chicken cooks evenly.

• Serve with fluffed-up rice and salad – perfect, yet so simple!

Healthy swap! *Reduce the saturated fat of the dish by swapping chicken for turkey.*

---

1 lemongrass stalk
1–2 chillies, (deseeded if you don't want it too hot)
2–3 garlic cloves, peeled
2cm piece of ginger, peeled
Small handful of coriander leaves
2 tbsp olive oil
Juice and zest of 1 lime
4 skinless chicken breasts, cut into large chunks
8–10 cherry tomatoes (optional)
1 red pepper, cut into wedges (optional)
Boiled fluffy rice and salad, to serve

Spicy chicken

3 tbsp olive oil

3 tbsp natural
Greek yoghurt (I
use Total)

1–2 chillies,
(deseeded if you
don't want it too
hot)

3 cloves of garlic,
peeled

1 tsp ground
cinnamon

1 tsp ground
coriander

2 tsp paprika

2 tsp allspice

2 tbsp agave syrup

Juice and zest of 1
lime

Small handful of
coriander leaves,
finely chopped

Salt and freshly
ground black
pepper

4–6 chicken breasts

Boiled rice, to serve

*This dish has a slight earthy, warming Moroccan flavour. I
really love it. You can serve the chicken on a bed of rice or
couscous. Simply whiz up the spices, leave to marinate with
the chicken, then cook for 20–30 minutes. Delicious.*

• Add all the ingredients, apart from the chicken, to a
food processor. Whiz to form a paste.

• Place the mixture into a plastic food bag. Score the
chicken breasts using a sharp knife and add to the
marinade. Secure the bag and shake to coat the
chicken pieces.

• Leave to marinate in the fridge overnight or for at
least 2–3 hours.

• When ready to cook, tip the contents into a greased
ovenproof dish.

• Preheat the halogen oven to 200°C or use the
preheat setting.

• Place on the high rack and cook for 20–30 minutes
until the chicken is cooked through.

• Serve on a bed of rice.

• For those who are nervous about cooking rice, here
are some simple tips. Choose the rice (basmati or
long-grain both work well for this dish). I normally use
$1^1/2$ cups of water to each cup of rice. Bring to the
boil, then simmer for 5 minutes. Cover, remove from
the heat and leave to stand for 10–15 minutes. Fluff
up the rice using a fork before serving. I like to cook
rice with frozen peas, chopped onions and peppers for
a bit of variety. You can also add some flavours such as
turmeric or pilau rice spices.

---

*Healthy swap! As with all chicken dishes, you can swap
chicken for turkey to reduce the saturated fat.*

Healthy chicken Kiev

Chicken Kiev is incredibly tasty but also very rich. This version gives you the same great taste but without the butter. You can prepare the chicken breasts in advance and can even freeze them uncooked.

• Using a sharp knife, cut a pocket into each chicken breast. Fill the pockets with the cream cheese, making sure not to overfill them as you don't want the filling bursting out when cooking. Secure the pockets with a cocktail stick.

• In a bowl, mix the breadcrumbs, oats, parsley, Parmesan and seasoning.

• Brush each chicken breast with beaten egg before dipping into the breadcrumb mixture. Ensure the chicken is evenly coated, then place on a greased baking tray.

• Place on the high rack and cook at 210°C for 20–25 minutes until golden.

• Serve with a salad.

4 skinless chicken
   breasts
200g garlic and
   herb low-fat
   cream cheese
75g wholemeal
   breadcrumbs
50g oats
1 tbsp freshly
   chopped parsley
30g Parmesan
   cheese, grated
Salt and freshly
   ground black
   pepper
1 large egg, beaten
Olive oil
Salad, to serve

Parma-wrapped chilli chicken

2–3 tbsp quark or
low-fat cream
cheese
1 red chilli, finely
chopped
(deseeded if you
don't want it too
hot)
1 tsp chilli powder
Few drops of
Tabasco sauce, to
taste (optional)
Salt and freshly
ground black
pepper
4 skinless chicken
breasts
4–8 slices of Parma
ham
Olive oil

A very simple dish that takes minutes to prepare.

• Preheat the halogen oven to 200°C or use the preheat setting.

• Place the quark or cream cheese in a bowl and mix the chilli, chilli powder and Tabasco sauce until combined. Season to taste.

• Using a sharp knife, make a slit in each chicken breast to form a pocket. Stuff the pockets with the creamed mixture.

• Wrap one or two slices of Parma ham around the chicken. Place, seam down, on a greased ovenproof dish. Season to taste.

• Place on the low rack and cook for 20–30 minutes until the chicken is cooked through.

• Serve with steamed green vegetables and sweet potato chips.

Did you know? *Chillies contain capsaicin, which helps lower blood sugars.*

Mustard chicken rolls

*The simplest recipes are often the best and this is no
exception – I use wholegrain mustard as I like the grainy
texture but it works just as well with Dijon mustard.*

• Wash the chicken before cutting the breasts in half
horizontally.

• Place the breasts on a sheet of greaseproof paper or
clingfilm. Use a rolling pin or meat mallet to flatten
the chicken until thin.

• In a bowl, mix the cream cheese with the mustard
and chives, and season with black pepper. Spread the
mixture over the flattened breasts.

• Carefully roll each breast up like a Swiss roll and
secure with a wooden cocktail stick (ideally soaked in
water).

• Place on a greased browning tray.

• Place on the high rack and cook at 200°C for 20–30
minutes until cooked through and golden.

• Serve with boiled new potatoes and seasonal
vegetables.

2–3 skinless
  chicken breasts
150g low-fat cream
  cheese
1 tbsp wholegrain
  mustard
2–3 tsp chopped
  chives
Freshly ground
  black pepper
Olive oil
Boiled new
  potatoes and
  seasonal
  vegetables, to
  serve

Coriander chicken

·Handful of fresh
coriander
Juice and zest of 1
lemon
3 cloves of garlic,
peeled
1 tsp black
peppercorns
2–3 tbsp olive oil
4–6 skinless
chicken pieces
1 red onion, peeled
and sliced
Savoury rice and
green salad, to
serve

You need to prepare this dish in advance as the chicken really benefits from being marinated.

• Whiz the coriander, lemon juice and zest, garlic, peppercorns and olive oil in a food processor.

• Score the chicken using a sharp knife – this helps the marinade soak into the chicken.

• Place the chicken pieces in a plastic food bag.

• Pour in the marinade, secure and combine well. Marinate in the fridge overnight or for at least 3–4 hours.

• When ready to cook, bring the chicken to room temperature.

• Grease an ovenproof dish and spread over the onion.

• Add the chicken pieces, including the marinade.

• Place on the high rack and cook at 200°C for 20–25 minutes. Cooking times will vary depending on the size and cuts of chicken you're using.

• Serve with savoury rice and green salad.

Did you know? *Brown rice is a great source of energy. It is high in magnesium and manganese, phytoestrogens and B vitamins. It really pays to swap white rice for brown!*

Grilled Indian chicken

These chicken breasts are sticky and spicy – you can add more chillies to give a bigger hit if you like things hot. Serve with pilau rice and vegetables for a delicious yet light meal.

• Score the chicken breasts using a sharp knife – this helps the paste adhere to the chicken.

• In a mini processor, combine the chillies, curry powder, oil and mango chutney.

• Spread the paste over the chicken and leave to marinate for at least 2–3 hours in the fridge (or overnight if you prefer, but bring back up to room temperature before cooking). When ready to cook, place the chicken on a baking tray.

• Place on the high rack (or grill rack if you have one) and grill at 235°C for about 8 minutes on each side, turning and basting with the marinade as you cook.

• Serve on a bed of pilau rice and vegetables.

4 skinless chicken
  breasts
1–2 chillies
  (deseeded if you
  don't want it too
  hot)
1 tsp hot curry
  powder
1 tsp olive oil
2–3 tbsp mango
  chutney
Pilau rice and
  vegetables, to
  serve

Chicken fricassee

Olive oil
500g skinless
   chicken breasts,
   cut into chunks
2 large red onions,
   peeled and
   roughly chopped
3 cloves of garlic,
   peeled and
   roughly chopped
2 green, yellow, red
   or orange
   peppers, thickly
   sliced
2 large carrots,
   peeled and cut
   into slices or
   batons
80g button
   mushrooms
400ml hot chicken
   stock (ideally
   homemade, if
   not use low-salt
   chicken stock)
1 tsp paprika
$^1/_2$ tsp dried parsley
2–3 sprigs of fresh
   thyme
2 bay leaves
Salt and freshly
   ground black
   pepper

My mum is a great cook and this is another of her recipes. She is a big fan of the halogen oven and spends her time convincing all her friends to buy one!

● Spray a large hob-proof casserole dish with olive oil, making sure the dish fits in your halogen oven. If you don't have one, use a sauté pan instead and transfer the contents into a casserole dish before placing in the oven.

● Cook the chicken until it turns white on all sides.

● Stir in all the remaining ingredients, season to taste and cook for a further 5–8 minutes.

● Place on the low rack and cook at 190°C for 30 minutes, or until the chicken is cooked through.

● Serve immediately.

Did you know? *I use red onions in most of my recipes are they contain great nutrients, like quercetin, more so than regular onions. It has been suggested that red onions have cancer-fighting properties (as have green tea, turmeric, garlic and broccoli). Red onions also contain allicin, which helps fight disease and can help lower blood pressure.*

Roasted one-pot chicken with sweet potato and squash

*Roasted sweet potato and squash have fantastic flavours –
add some garlic and chilli and you have a divine meal. Feel
free to add more chilli to taste, or for extra flavour use chilli
oil instead of olive oil.*

• Place the onions, garlic, chilli, sweet potatoes and
squash on a roasting tin and spray with olive oil or
chilli oil. Season with black pepper.

• Toss well and spray again if needed.

• Sprinkle with half the paprika. Place on the low rack
and cook at 210°C for 10 minutes.

• Add the chicken and cherry tomatoes. Spray again
with oil and sprinkle with the remaining paprika.

• Bake for a further 35–45 minutes until the chicken is
cooked through.

• Serve with a green salad.

2 large red onions,
  peeled and cut
  into wedges
4 cloves of garlic,
  peeled and left
  whole
1 chilli, finely sliced
3 sweet potatoes,
  skins on, cut into
  thick chunks
1 small squash, skin
  on, cut into
  chunks
Spray of olive oil or
  drizzle of chilli oil
Freshly ground
  black pepper
4 tsp paprika
4 chicken breasts
12 cherry tomatoes
Green salad, to
  serve

Healthy chicken nuggets

Olive oil, for
greasing
200g instant (pre-
cooked) polenta
flour
3 eggs, beaten
Freshly ground
black pepper
4 tbsp sesame
seeds
3–4 skinless,
boneless chicken
breasts, cut into
strips or chunks

*Children love chicken nuggets but if they are processed they
are high in fat and salt. These nuggets can be made in
minutes. Polenta flour is really versatile and makes a
fantastic crispy coating. Use turkey breasts instead of
chicken if you prefer.*

● Thoroughly grease and line a baking tray, as the
batter will stick to it.

● Mix the batter ingredients in a bowl, along with
210ml water. Dip in the chicken pieces, making sure
they are evenly coated in the batter. Place on the
baking tray.

● Place on the high rack and cook at 200°C for 15–20
minutes until cooked through and golden.

Lemon and honey chicken

This is a lovely lemony chicken with a slightly sticky coating. You can add garlic for an additional kick but I love the simplicity of just the lemon.

• Score the chicken using a sharp knife – this helps the flavours soak into the chicken.

• Place the chicken on a greased ovenproof dish.

• Place the lemon juice, zest, butter and honey together in a saucepan and heat gently until combined. Season with black pepper and add the lemon thyme.

• Pour over the chicken.

• Place the chicken on the high rack and cook at 200°C for 20–25 minutes, or until cooked through.

• Serve with boiled new potatoes and a green salad.

4 skinless chicken
   fillets
Olive oil, for
   greasing
Juice and zest of
   2–3 lemons
2 tbsp butter
3 tbsp honey
Freshly ground
   black pepper
Small handful of
   lemon thyme
Boiled new
   potatoes and
   green salad, to
   serve

Fish

It's really important to include as much oily fish as possible in your diet. With this in mind, I have tried to offer an extensive range of recipe ideas. Fish tastes delicious and is really healthy, so give it a go!

Oily fish is packed with essential Omega-3 and should be included in at least three meals a week. Choose from mackerel, trout, salmon, sardines, pilchards and herring.

If you don't like oily fish, consider taking a daily supplement, but buy these from reputable companies such as Nutrigold, Solgar or Patrick Holford. Cod liver oil is not the same as Omega-3-rich fish oil, so don't buy it. I am really impressed with krill oil. This is a new, more powerful fish-oil supplement. Some manufacturers mix krill oil with fish oil – you can tell because pure krill oil will not leave a fishy aftertaste in your mouth – or fishy burps! Research suggests it provides a substantially greater reduction of fat in the heart and liver than Omega-3 fish oil, while also helping to reduce high blood pressure, lower cholesterol and possibly protect against osteoporosis. It has also been noted to help reduce wrinkles – my kind of supplement!

Did you know? *Oily fish has been shown to help protect from Alzheimer's and heart disease, and can improve joint health.*

Chilli and spring onion mackerel

Serves

4

4 tbsp olive oil

3 cloves of garlic, peeled and finely chopped

1–2 red chillies, finely chopped (deseeded if you don't want it too hot)

5 spring onions, finely chopped

Juice and zest of 1 lemon

Salt and freshly ground black pepper

4 mackerel, cleaned, heads removed and gutted

Crusty bread and green salad, to serve

This recipe uses omega-rich mackerel. A great summer dish, perfect for alfresco dining.

• Place the oil, garlic, chillies, spring onions and lemon juice and zest in a bowl and combine well. Season to taste.

• Score the fish on both sides using a sharp knife, making regular slits to expose the flesh.

• Place the fish on a baking tray. Spoon some of the sauce over the fish, rubbing it into the skin.

• Place on the grill rack (see p.3) and grill at 240°C for about 8 minutes on each side (cooking times will vary depending on the size and thickness of the fish), basting with more sauce.

• Remove from the oven and place the fish on warmed plates ready to serve. Pour the remaining juice over the fish. Serve with crusty bread and a green salad.

Did you know? *Mackerel is rich in Omega-3, vitamins D and B12, as well as selenium and phosphorus.*

Baked coley, fennel and red onion

Fennel features prominently in Mediterranean cuisine and works really well with fish. You could use cod or pollack instead of coley in this recipe if you prefer.

• Season the fish fillets and squeeze over a little lemon juice. Set aside until needed.

• Place the fennel, onions, garlic and one lemon cut into wedges in a roasting or baking tray. Spray with olive oil.

• Place on the low rack and cook at 190°C for 15 minutes.

• Place the fish fillets on top of the vegetables. Squeeze the juice of the remaining lemon and drizzle over the dish. Season to taste. Cover securely with foil and bake for a further 15–20 minutes, or until the fish is thoroughly cooked and flakes easily (cooking times will vary depending on the size and thickness of the fillets).

• Remove the foil and serve with steamed new potatoes and a fresh green salad.

Did you know? *It has been suggested that red onions have cancer-fighting properties (as have green tea, turmeric, garlic and broccoli). Red onions also contain allicin, which helps fight disease and can help lower blood pressure.*

2–4 coley fillets, cleaned, heads removed and gutted
Salt and freshly ground black pepper
2 lemons
1 large or 2 small fennel bulbs, sliced
2 red onions, peeled and sliced
2–3 cloves of garlic, peeled and finely sliced
Olive oil
Steamed new potatoes and green salad, to serve

Foil-baked salmon with mango salsa

4 salmon fillets
2 lemons (1 sliced,
  $^1/_2$ cut into
  wedges, juice of
  $^1/_2$)
Salt and freshly
  ground black
  pepper
Generous handful
  of rocket, lambs
  leaf, watercress
  or mixed salad
  leaves for each
  serving
$^1/_2$ cucumber, diced
Small handful of
  chopped
  coriander

For the salsa
1 ripe mango
1 ripe avocado
1 red chilli, finely
  chopped
6 spring onions,
  finely chopped
1 yellow pepper,
  diced
Juice and zest of 1
  lime

Baked fish is so simple and delicious. I love the freshness of the salsa combined with the fish and peppery salad leaves.

• Place the salmon fillets in the centre of a piece of foil. Add one or two slices of lemon on top of each fillet. Add a squeeze of lemon juice and season to taste. Wrap and place on a baking tray.

• Place on the low rack and cook at 190°C for 15–20 minutes, or until cooked to your liking (cooking times will vary depending on the size and thickness of the fillets).

• Meanwhile, make the salsa. Place all the ingredients in a bowl and mash/mix well.

• Just before serving, place the salad leaves and coriander on serving plates. Place the salmon on the top and drizzle with the salsa. Serve with the remaining half-lemon on the side.

Did you know? *Some studies have shown that Omega-3-rich salmon can keep you fuller for longer by lowering the hunger hormone leptin.*

Spicy cod

This is really simple but tastes amazing. You can make the paste in advance and store it in the fridge ready to use.

• Put all the ingredients, apart from the cod, in a food processor. Blend to form a smooth paste. If the paste looks too dry add a dash of olive oil and a little more lime juice. If the lime seems reluctant to give up any juice, roll it for a couple of minutes or heat it up gently in the microwave for 30 seconds before juicing.

• Wash the cod fillets and place them in a greased ovenproof dish. Spread the paste evenly on top of the fillets. Cover with clingfilm and refrigerate for at least 30 minutes.

• When you are ready to cook, remove the clingfilm and place the dish on the high rack. Cook at 190°C for 15–20 minutes until the fish is cooked through.

• Serve with a lovely herb and green leafy salad.

2–3 tbsp olive oil
$^1/_2$–1 chilli, deseeded
2–3 cloves of garlic, peeled
2cm piece of fresh ginger, peeled
$^1/_2$ tsp turmeric
1–2 tsp sweet curry powder
Small handful each of fresh coriander and fresh mint
Juice and zest of 1 lime
Olive oil (optional)
4 cod fillets, skinned
Herb and green leafy salad

400g fresh or
canned salmon
300g potatoes,
peeled, cooked
and mashed
3–4 spring onions,
very finely
chopped
Juice of $^1/_2$ lemon
2–3 tsp each of
fresh dill and
tarragon
Freshly ground
black pepper
1 egg, beaten
Olive oil or chilli oil
Boiled new
potatoes and
green salad, to
serve

Salmon fishcakes

Fishcakes are so easy to make – get the kids involved as they love getting their hands dirty. If you're using leftover mashed potato and find it a little hard to mix with, just warm it gently and add a little milk or low-fat spread and re-mash.

• Mix the salmon, potatoes, spring onions, lemon juice and herbs together in a bowl. Season to taste and stir in the egg to bind.

• Form the mixture into four large or eight small cakes, place on baking parchment and refrigerate for 10 minutes.

• Remove from the fridge, brush with a light coating of olive oil, or chilli oil if you like a bit of a kick.

• Place on the high rack (or grill rack if you have one) and grill on both sides at 250°C for 8–10 minutes. Wait until the cakes have cooked on one side before turning them as they are quite fragile.

• Serve with boiled new potatoes and green salad.

Did you know? *Salmon is rich in Omega-3, a good source of protein, and is packed with vitamins, minerals and micronutrients.*

Wholemeal breaded fish fillets

You can use any fish for this recipe. Speak to your fishmonger for the best deals. Remember to opt for Omega-3-rich fish if you can.

• Place breadcrumbs, oats, chives, parsley, Parmesan and lemon zest in a bowl and combine well.

• Spread the top of the fillets with cream cheese.

• Dip into the breaded mixture ensuring the fillets are well coated and then place on a greased or lined baking tray.

• Place on the high rack at 190°C and bake for 10–15 minutes.

• Serve with boiled new potatoes and a salad.

50g home-prepared
  wholemeal
  breadcrumbs
1 tbsp oats
1 tbsp chives
1 tbsp chopped
  parsley
1 tbsp grated
  Parmesan cheese
Zest of 1 lemon
4 fish fillets
4–5 tsp low-fat
  cream cheese
Boiled new
  potatoes and
  salad, to serve

Baked salmon with minted salsa and roasted tomatoes

4 salmon fillets
2 lemons (1 sliced,
   $^1/_2$ cut into
   wedges, juice of
   $^1/_2$)
Salt and freshly
   ground black
   pepper
12 vine tomatoes
Olive oil

For the salsa
1 red onion, peeled
   and diced
1 ripe avocado,
   diced
1 red chilli, finely
   chopped
1 red pepper, diced
Juice and zest of 1
   lime
$^1/_4$ cucumber, diced
Small handful of
   chopped mint
   leaves, plus extra
   to serve
Extra-virgin olive oil
1 lime, cut into
   wedges, to serve

Salmon is rich in Omega-3, a good source of protein and packed with vitamins, minerals and micronutrients.

• Place the salmon fillets in the centre of a piece of foil. Add one or two slices of lemon on top of each fillet. Add a squeeze of lemon juice and season to taste. Wrap and place on a baking tray.

• Place the tomatoes on a separate baking tray, with their stalks intact. Drizzle with a little olive oil, and season.

• Place the salmon on the low rack and cook at 190°C for 15–20 minutes, or until cooked to your liking. Add the tomatoes 10 minutes later and leave in the oven until the salmon is cooked.

• Meanwhile, make the salsa. Place all the ingredients, apart from the olive oil, in a bowl and mix well.

• Drizzle with olive oil and an extra squeeze of lime.

• Place the salmon on warmed plates with the baked tomatoes. Top with the salsa and finish with a drizzle of extra-virgin olive oil and a few mint leaves. Serve with a lime wedge on the side.

Did you know? *Avocados contain oleic acid, which has been shown to help reduce cholesterol. They are also high in fibre and rich in potassium.*

Cod, tomato and red pepper kebabs

You can use any fish for this dish. I have chosen cod as it is a family favourite, but feel free to experiment. If you are using wooden skewers, remember to soak them overnight before use or they will burn. You can use metal skewers too, but be careful as they get very hot.

• In a bowl mix the yoghurt, mint, and lime juice and zest together. Season with black pepper.

• Carefully thread a chunk of fish, a bay leaf, a cherry tomato and a chunk of red pepper onto a skewer. Repeat until the skewers are filled. You should have about four skewers in total.

• Using a pastry brush, brush the cod pieces with the yoghurt mixture, ensuring they are evenly coated.

• Place the skewers directly on the grill rack (see p.3) and grill at 250°C for 8–10 minutes, or until the fish is cooked to your liking, turning regularly to ensure an even cook. Cooking times will vary depending on the size and thickness of the fillets and how close to the heat they are.

• Serve immediately on a bed of fragrant rice.

4–5 tbsp fat-free Greek yoghurt

Small handful of fresh mint, finely chopped

Juice and zest of 1/2 lime

Freshly ground black pepper

3–4 cod fillets, skinned and cut into chunks

Handful of bay leaves

12–16 cherry tomatoes

2–3 red peppers, cut into thick chunks

Fragrant rice, to serve

Haddock bake

2 large potatoes,
   peeled and diced
2 sweet potatoes,
   peeled and diced
2 carrots, peeled
   and diced
3 eggs
150ml skimmed
   milk
Salt and freshly
   ground black
   pepper
500g haddock
   pieces
200g fat-free Greek
   yoghurt
150g quark or low-
   fat cream cheese
Juice and zest of
   $^1/_2$ lemon
1 tbsp chopped
   fresh parsley
Salad or steamed
   green
   vegetables, to
   serve

This is great comfort food. The creamy sauce combined with the mash are perfect when you want a tasty supper.

• Place the potatoes, sweet potatoes and carrots in a steamer and steam until soft. Add the eggs to the boiling water of the steamer and cook for 6 minutes. Remove and place in cold water to cool. Mash the potatoes and carrots with half the milk and season to taste.

• Steam the haddock for 8–10 minutes until cooked.

• Flake the haddock into an ovenproof dish. Shell the eggs and cut them into quarters. Add them to the fish.

• In a bowl, mix the yoghurt, quark or cream cheese, the remaining milk, and lemon juice and zest together. Add the parsley and season to taste with black pepper. Pour over the haddock.

• Spread the mash on top of the haddock.

• Place on the low rack and cook at 180°C for 20 minutes, until piping hot.

• Serve with a salad or steamed green vegetables.

Did you know? *You are more likely to suffer from depression if you are low in vitamin B12. Great sources of vitamin B12 include eggs, shellfish, haddock, trout and salmon. If you do suffer from low mood or depression, it would be well worth taking a course of a good-quality B-complex (a range of B vitamins).*

Simple fish kebabs

Lovely for alfresco dining. Serve with rice and a selection of salads. Remember, if you are using wooden skewers, to soak them for a few hours before using them.

• Mix all the ingredients together, apart from the fish, and season with black pepper.

• Place the fish in a bowl and pour over the marinade.

• Leave to marinate for at least 45 minutes.

• Thread the fish onto four skewers.

• Place the kebabs on a baking tray on the high rack and grill at 235°C for about 10 minutes, turning regularly to ensure an even cook. Brush on more marinade as you cook.

2 tbsp olive oil
Juice and zest of 1 lemon
1 tbsp wholegrain mustard
1–2 cloves of garlic, peeled (optional)
Freshly ground black pepper
400g fish pieces (you can use haddock, cod, monkfish or prawns)

Sardines with tomato and herbs

1–2 red onions,
peeled and diced
8 tomatoes, halved
2 cloves of garlic,
peeled and
roughly chopped
2 sprigs of rosemary
2 sprigs of thyme
Olive oil
8 sardines, cleaned
and heads
removed
Juice of 1 lemon
Salt and freshly
ground black
pepper

Forget the canned variety, use fresh sardines instead – if you can get them straight off the boat, even better! They work brilliantly with the herb topping and the flavours are amazing together.

• Place the onions, tomatoes, garlic and herbs in an ovenproof dish. Drizzle with olive oil and combine well.

• Place on the high rack and cook at 200°C for 15 minutes.

• Meanwhile, wash the sardines. Score diagonal strips across the skin of each sardine using a sharp knife. Squeeze over some lemon juice and season to taste. Place on a baking tray.

• Remove the vegetables from the high rack, stir to combine and burst the tomatoes before placing on the base of the halogen to keep warm.

• Place the sardines on the high rack and grill at 235°C on both sides for 8–10 minutes until cooked.

• Serve the fish with the onion, tomato and herb mixture drizzled over.

Did you know? *Sardines are a great source of Omega-3 and vitamin D.*

Thai cod parcels

If you like the Thai flavours you will love this dish. You can opt for pollack or a similar white fish instead of cod if you prefer.

• In a bowl mix the lime juice and zest, soy sauce, fish sauce, garlic and ginger.

• Add the chillies, lemongrass and spring onions to the bowl and marinate for 20 minutes.

• Place the fillets onto four individual foil squares. Sprinkle with the vegetables and drizzle with a little of the marinade before sealing to make parcels.

• Place on the low rack and cook at 190°C for 20–25 minutes, or until cooked through.

• Serve with a lovely green salad.

Did you know? *Good sources of Omega-3 include mackerel, sardines, salmon, fresh tuna, walnuts, brazil nuts, hazelnuts, pecans, sesame seeds and flax oil.*

Juice and zest of 1 lime
2 tbsp light soy sauce
1 tbsp fish sauce
2 cloves of garlic, peeled and finely chopped
2.5cm piece of ginger, peeled and finely chopped
1–2 chillies, finely chopped
2 lemongrass stalks, finely cut lengthways
4 spring onions, finely sliced lengthways
4 cod fillets
Green salad, to serve

300g white fish
    fillets (such as
    cod or pollack)
100g wholemeal
    breadcrumbs
50g oats
1 carrot, peeled and
    grated
Salt and freshly
    ground black
    pepper
1 large egg, beaten

Golden oat crunch fish fingers

These fish fingers are simple to make and can even be frozen. They are perfect for children! Try to get away from the yucky processed fish fingers and encourage them to go for the healthier option.

• Cut the fish fillets into thick fingers.

• In a bowl, mix the breadcrumbs, oats and carrot, and season to taste.

• Brush the fish fingers with egg, then dip into the breadcrumb mixture, ensuring they are evenly coated.

• Place the fingers on a greased baking tray.

• You can either freeze them until needed or bake on the high rack, in a preheated halogen oven set to 210°C, for 15 minutes, turning once.

• Serve immediately.

Did you know? The latest Health Survey for England (HSE) data shows that in 2009 almost a quarter of adults – 22 per cent of men and 24 per cent of women – were obese. 66 per cent of men and 57 per cent of women were overweight, including obese.

Honeyed salmon and asparagus parcels

My mum passed on this recipe, which is truly delicious and so simple. Yes, it is another parcel recipe but really, why not? They are so simple and save on washing up. Try to buy the asparagus when in season – the taste of fresh British asparagus is second to none.

• Mix the melted butter, honey, mustard and lemon zest together. Season with black pepper.

• Place an equal number of asparagus spears onto four individual foil squares. (You also may want to line the foil with parchment, or you can buy foil backed with parchment from Lakeland).

• Place the salmon fillets on top of the asparagus and drizzle with honey mixture.

• Seal the foil parcels securely.

• Place the parcels on the low rack and cook at 210°C for 20–25 minutes, or until the fish flakes easily.

• Serve with boiled new potatoes and green seasonal vegetables.

20g butter or low-fat spread, melted
3 tbsp runny honey
1 tbsp Dijon mustard
Zest of $1/2$ lemon
Freshly ground black pepper
250g fresh asparagus, trimmed
4 salmon fillets
Boiled new potatoes and seasonal vegetables, to serve

Tuna steak with spicy salsa

2 red peppers,
    diced
1 chilli, diced
$1/2$ cucumber, diced
1 red onion, peeled
    and diced
3 tomatoes, diced
2–3 cloves of garlic,
    peeled and
    crushed
Small handful of
    flat-leaf parsley,
    chopped
1 tsp balsamic
    vinegar
3 tbsp olive oil, plus
    extra
Freshly ground
    black pepper
4 tuna steaks
Juice of $1/2$ lemon
Asparagus and
    boiled new
    potatoes, to
    serve

A delicious meal served on its own or with asparagus and new potatoes.

● In a bowl, mix the chopped vegetables, garlic, parsley, balsamic vinegar and olive oil, and season with black pepper.

● Rub a little olive oil into the tuna steaks. Drizzle with lemon juice and season with black pepper.

● Place on the grill rack (see p.3) and grill at 250°C for 3–4 minutes on each side, or until done to your liking. Cooking times will vary depending on the thickness of the steaks and how close to the heat they are.

● Place on warmed plates and spoon over the salsa.

● Serve with asparagus and boiled new potatoes.

Did you know? *Flavonoids are found in tea, red wine, onions and citrus fruits; they help protect the immune system and have antiviral and antibacterial properties.*

Easy chilli, garlic and ginger baked prawns

A really simple meal. Prepare in advance and keep in the fridge ready to parcel up when required.

• In a large bowl, mix the garlic, ginger, spring onions, chillies, lemongrass, lemon juice and zest, olive oil, oyster sauce and 2–3 tablespoons of water together. Season to taste.

• Add the coriander, green beans and prawns, and toss until thoroughly mixed.

• Line a large piece of foil (make sure it is big enough) with parchment (or you can buy foil backed with parchment from Lakeland). Spray or brush with olive oil.

• Bring up the sides of the foil to form a bowl shape. I find sitting the foil in a bowl helps keep the shape and avoids mess.

• Carefully pour or spoon the mixture into the foil. Bring up the sides and secure to form a parcel.

• Place on the low rack and cook at 200°C for 18–25 minutes, depending on the size of the prawns.

• Remove from the oven and leave to rest for 5 minutes before transferring to a large warmed serving dish. Serve with crusty bread or on a bed of fluffy rice.

2–3 cloves of garlic, peeled
3cm piece of ginger, peeled and finely chopped
8 spring onions, finely chopped
1–2 chillies, finely chopped
1 lemongrass stalk, peeled and finely chopped
Juice and zest of 1 large lemon
2 tbsp olive oil, plus extra for spraying/brushing
1 tbsp oyster sauce
Salt and freshly ground pepper
Handful of coriander leaves, finely chopped
150g green beans, trimmed and halved
1kg raw king or tiger prawns, peeled
Crusty bread or fluffy rice, to serve

Mackerel bake

1kg new potatoes
4 mackerel fillets
1 onion, peeled and
    sliced
300g low-fat crème
    fraîche
300g quark
200ml skimmed
    milk
2 tbsp wholegrain
    mustard
Salt and freshly
    ground black
    pepper
100g breadcrumbs
50g oats
50g low-fat mature
    cheese (I use
    Cheddar), grated
Salad, to serve

If you are looking for a comforting supper, this is the one for you. Use raw and not smoked mackerel.

• Boil or steam the new potatoes until almost soft. When cooked, drain and cut into thick slices.

• Grease an ovenproof dish (I use a deep Pyrex dish). Place a layer of potato on the base, followed by some flaked mackerel and onion. Repeat, finishing with a layer of potato.

• In a bowl, combine the crème fraîche and quark with the milk and mustard. Season to taste and pour over the layers.

• In a separate bowl, combine the breadcrumbs, oats and cheese, and sprinkle on top of the dish. Season with black pepper.

• Place on the high rack and cook at 200°C for 20–25 minutes until golden and bubbling.

• Serve with salad for a fabulous supper.

Did you know? Over 60 per cent of adults in the UK have cholesterol levels above the safe limit, which can lead to coronary heart disease and strokes. Eating a diet rich in fibre, such as oats and wholegrains, can help, as well as a diet rich in Omega-3, which can be found in mackerel, salmon, sardines or tuna.

Vegetable and halibut pot roast

This simple one-pot can be prepared in advance, stored covered in the fridge and popped into the oven when you are ready to eat.

• Drizzle a deep baking tray with olive oil. Place the fish fillets, onions, red peppers, garlic and cherry tomatoes in the tray and combine until evenly distributed.

• Add the capers and thyme and drizzle again with olive oil. Finish with a sprinkle of balsamic vinegar and season with black pepper.

• Cover the tray with foil, making sure it is secure.

• Place on the high rack and cook at 200°C for 20 minutes.

• Remove the foil and cook for a further 5 minutes. Serve with boiled new potatoes.

Did you know? *Onions and garlic contain allicin, which helps fight disease and can help lower blood pressure.*

Olive oil
4 halibut fillets
2 red onions, peeled and cut into wedges
2 red peppers, cut into thick slices or wedges
3–4 cloves of garlic, peeled and roughly chopped
12–16 cherry tomatoes
2 tbsp capers
3 sprigs of thyme
Balsamic vinegar
Freshly ground black pepper
Boiled new potatoes, to serve

4 salmon fillets
Juice and zest of 1
  lemon
Salt and freshly
  ground black
  pepper
1kg new potatoes,
  halved
Small bunch of
  spring onions,
  finely chopped
Small bunch of
  chives, finely
  chopped
150g fat-free Greek
  yoghurt
1–2 tbsp lemon
  juice
Handful of chopped
  parsley
1/2 cucumber, finely
  sliced
Leafy salad, to
  serve

Baked salmon with new potato salad and yoghurt dressing

This can be prepared in advance.

• Place the salmon fillets on a large square of foil, drizzle with the lemon juice, scatter with lemon zest and season with black pepper. Seal the parcel, place it on a baking tray and leave until ready to cook.

• Place on the low rack and cook at 200°C for 15–20 minutes, or to your liking.

• Meanwhile, steam the potatoes until just soft.

• Tip them into a bowl and add the spring onions and chives.

• In a bowl mix the yoghurt, lemon juice and parsley, and season to taste.

• Pour two-thirds of the yoghurt dressing in with the potatoes, reserving the rest to pour on top of the salmon.

• Place the potatoes onto warmed plates, top with a few slices of cucumber, followed by the salmon. Drizzle with remaining yoghurt dressing.

• Serve with a leafy salad.

Salmon, sweet potato and chilli fishcakes

These fishcakes are really delicious. Add as much chilli as you dare – if you're really brave add the seeds to create lovely fiery fishcakes.

• Mix the fish, sweet potatoes, spring onions, chillies, cumin, lemon juice and coriander together in a bowl. Add a little beaten egg to bind if necessary. Season to taste.

• Form the mixture into cakes. If it is too wet, add a little plain flour. Place on a piece of greased baking parchment and chill in the fridge for 10 minutes.

• Preheat the halogen oven to 250°C or use the preheat setting.

• Remove the cakes from the fridge and brush with a light coating of olive oil.

• Place on the high rack either on a baking tray or browning pan or directly on the rack.

• Grill the cakes for 5–6 minutes on each side, turning halfway through to ensure even cooking.

• Serve with a lovely salad and a chilli dip.

300g fresh or canned salmon

350g sweet potatoes, peeled, steamed or boiled, and mashed

3–4 spring onions, including green stalks, finely chopped

2 chillies, finely chopped

1 tsp ground cumin

1 tbsp lemon juice

Small handful of coriander leaves, finely chopped

1 egg, beaten

Salt and freshly ground black pepper

Plain flour (if needed)

Olive oil

Salad and chilli dip, to serve

Grilled mackerel

4 mackerel,
cleaned, gutted,
heads and tails
removed
Olive oil
Salt and freshly
ground black
pepper
2–3 tbsp
horseradish
Juice and zest of 1
lemon
1 onion, peeled and
finely chopped
Small handful each
of fresh thyme
and fresh parsley,
finely chopped
1–2 tbsp low-fat
crème fraîche
(optional)
Boiled new
potatoes and
salad, to serve

Buy fresh mackerel – a great source of Omega-3.

• Score the fish on both sides using a sharp knife and brush with olive oil. Sprinkle with black pepper.

• Place on the grill rack (see p.3) and grill at 250°C for about 6 minutes on each side.

• Meanwhile, mix the remaining ingredients together in a bowl and season to taste. If you want a creamier sauce, add the crème fraîche.

• Place the fish onto warmed plates and add a spoonful of the sauce over the mackerel. Serve with boiled new potatoes and salad.

Grilled sardines with mustard dressing

A posh version of sardines on toast!

• In a bowl, mix the tomatoes with the garlic and sugar. Drizzle with a little olive oil and season to taste. Transfer to a baking tray.

• Place on the high rack and cook at 210°C for 10 minutes.

• Meanwhile, wash the fish, remove the heads and make a slit along one side from head to tail. Open out the fish and place it skin side up. Press along the backbone with the heel of your hand. Flip it over and carefully remove all the bones. Season with black pepper.

• Remove the tomatoes from the oven and set aside.

• Place the fish on a baking tray or directly on the grill rack and grill at 250°C for 3–4 minutes on each side. (Cooking times will vary depending on the size of the fish.) For the last few minutes of cooking, place the tomato mixture on the low rack to heat through, or reheat gently in a pan.

• Meanwhile, make the dressing. Mix the oil, mustard, sugar and lemon zest together. Season to taste.

• Place a large slice of crusty or French bread on warmed plates. Spoon the tomato mixture over the bread and top with the sardines. Drizzle with the mustard dressing and season to taste. Add some fresh herbs to garnish.

6 tomatoes, finely chopped
1–2 cloves of garlic, peeled
Pinch of sugar
Olive oil
Salt and freshly ground black pepper
8–12 sardines (allow 2–3 per person, depending on size)
4 slices of crusty or French bread
Fresh herbs, to garnish

For the dressing
2 tbsp olive oil
1 tbsp wholegrain mustard
1 tsp sugar, plus an extra pinch
Zest of 1 lemon

Salmon kebabs

1 large salmon fillet
2–3 tbsp runny
honey
Dash of soy sauce
2cm piece of
ginger, peeled
and finely grated
2 cloves of garlic,
peeled and
chopped
1 tbsp olive oil, plus
extra for
brushing
Salt and freshly
ground black
pepper
350g new potatoes,
steamed or
boiled
2 courgettes, cut
into thick chunks
1 red pepper, cut
into thick chunks
1 yellow pepper, cut
into thick chunks
Savoury rice, to
serve

Our British weather can be so unpredictable, so it's nice to know you can still make delicious kebabs without the barbecue.

• If you are using wooden skewers, soak them overnight. Cut the salmon into chunks and place in a bowl.

• In another bowl, mix the honey, soy sauce, ginger, garlic and olive oil together. Season to taste. Pour over the salmon and leave to marinate for 1 hour.

• When you are ready to cook, thread the potatoes, courgettes, salmon and peppers onto four skewers.

• Brush or spray with a little olive oil and season to taste. Place on a baking tray.

• Place on the high rack and grill at 250°C for 10–12 minutes, turning occasionally until thoroughly cooked.

• Serve with savoury rice.

Cod Romanesco

You can of course use any white fish fillet for this recipe. I usually prepare the Romanesco-style topping in advance.

• Place all the ingredients, apart from the cod and half the parsley, in a food processor and whiz until roughly combined.

• Spread a thick layer of the mixture over each fish fillet. Place in a greased ovenproof dish.

• Place on the low rack and cook at 190°C for about 20 minutes, or until the fish flakes easily (cooking times will vary depending on the size of the fillets).

• Serve with boiled new potatoes and French beans.

Did you know? *Potassium is found in many fruit and vegetables, including apricots, avocados, bananas, tomatoes, potatoes, spinach and mushrooms. It's also found in nuts and seeds, milk, baked beans, lentils, meat, poultry and fish.*

1–2 chillies, depending on taste

3 cloves of garlic, peeled

6–8 sun-dried tomatoes (soaked in oil), drained

$1/2$ tsp paprika

40g cashew nuts

2 tbsp olive oil (or the oil from the sun-dried tomatoes)

Small handful of fresh parsley

4 plump cod fillets

Boiled new potatoes and French beans, to serve

Light salmon and prawn pie

3 spring onions,
  finely chopped
450g fresh or
  canned salmon
  chunks
100g raw prawns
Juice and zest of
  $1/2$ lemon
200g low-fat crème
  fraîche
150g quark
Small handful of
  finely chopped
  parsley
Freshly ground
  black pepper
4–5 filo pastry
  sheets
Boiled new
  potatoes and
  green
  vegetables, to
  serve

Filo pastry is lower in fat than short or puff pastry. Don't place too much pastry on top of the fish – it will crisp up and give you a light topping.

• Place the spring onions, salmon and prawns in a deep ovenproof dish.

• In a bowl, mix the lemon juice and zest, crème fraîche and quark together. Stir in the parsley and season with black pepper.

• Pour over the fish and combine.

• Scrunch up the filo pastry and place randomly on top of the salmon.

• Place on the high rack and cook at 190°C for 20 minutes until golden.

• Serve with boiled new potatoes and green vegetables.

Easy salmon and watercress tart

I have called this a tart but really it's a cross between a frittata and a quiche. Delicious served hot or cold and perfect for alfresco dining. You can, of course, use a basic frittata recipe and add your own favourite ingredients. It works just as well with roasted vegetables or more traditional quiche-type flavours of bacon, onion and tomato.

• Place the vegetables and salmon in a bowl.

• In a jug mix the eggs, milk and polenta together. Add the lemon zest and season with black pepper.

• Pour the egg mixture over the salmon and combine well.

• Grease and line a 22–24cm springform cake tin with baking parchment.

• Pour the mixture into the tin.

• Place on the low rack and cook at 200°C for 35–45 minutes.

• Serve with a selection of salad leaves.

Did you know? *Gram for gram watercress contains more iron than spinach, more calcium than milk and more vitamin C than oranges. It is naturally low in fat and salt and brimming with more than 15 essential vitamins and minerals. New research also suggests that it could play an important role in cancer prevention.*

---

¹/₂ bunch of spring onions, finely chopped
2 handfuls of watercress
210g can salmon, drained and flaked into chunks
6 eggs, beaten
125ml skimmed milk
5 tbsp fine polenta
Zest of 1 lemon
Freshly ground black pepper
Salad, to serve

1 tsp coconut oil
1 red onion, peeled
   and finely
   chopped
2 cloves of garlic,
   peeled and
   crushed
1 red pepper, sliced
400g can cherry
   tomatoes
Handful of green or
   black olives,
   halved
1 tsp dried oregano
Small handful of
   fresh basil
2 tsp sun-dried
   tomato paste
$^1/_2$ tsp sugar
Pinch of salt and
   freshly ground
   black pepper
4 halibut steaks
Steamed new
   potatoes and
   green
   vegetables, to
   serve

Italian baked halibut

I love Italian flavours, and the combination of herbs with juicy tomatoes, olives and garlic. I used canned cherry tomatoes as they create a lovely sauce and nicer flavour, but you could use ordinary canned chopped tomatoes if you prefer.

• Place the coconut oil in a sauté pan and heat gently.

• Add the onion, garlic and red pepper, and cook for a few minutes to soften.

• Add the tomatoes, olives, herbs and tomato paste, and season with the sugar, salt and black pepper.

• Remove from the heat.

• Place the halibut steaks in a greased ovenproof dish and pour over the sauce.

• Place on the low rack and cook at 210°C for 15–18 minutes.

• Serve immediately with steamed new potatoes and green vegetables.

Pollack and vegetable casserole

You can use coley or sustainable cod instead of pollack in this recipe.

• Place the fillet chunks in a bowl and season with black pepper.

• In a blender, mix the oil, lemon juice and zest, coriander leaves, garlic, chilli, cumin, ground coriander and paprika. Whiz until smooth.

• Pour this over the fillet chunks, cover with clingfilm and leave to marinate for at least 2 hours or overnight.

• When you are ready to cook, heat a casserole dish (or sauté pan if your casserole dish is not hob-proof) on the hob. Spray with a little olive oil, then add the onion and peppers. Cook until they start to soften.

• Add the fish, including all the marinade, and cook for a further 5 minutes.

• Add all the remaining ingredients and simmer gently for 5 minutes on the hob before transferring to the low rack in the halogen oven. Cook at 180°C for 30–40 minutes.

• Garnish with a few sprigs of coriander before serving.

500g pollack fillets, cut into large chunks
Freshly ground black pepper
3 tbsp olive oil
Juice and zest of $1/2$ lemon
Small handful of coriander leaves, plus extra to garnish
3–4 cloves of garlic, peeled
1 chilli
1 tsp cumin
1 tsp ground coriander
3 tsp paprika
1 large red onion, peeled
1 red pepper, sliced
1 yellow pepper, sliced
300g new potatoes, halved
2 sweet potatoes, peeled and thickly diced
400g can chopped tomatoes
400g can chickpeas, drained
250ml hot fish stock

Salmon fish fingers

Olive oil, for
   greasing
200g polenta flour
3 eggs, beaten
Freshly ground
   black pepper
$1/2$ tsp turmeric
4 tbsp sesame
   seeds
400g salmon (or
   white fish fillets),
   cut into fingers

*You can use salmon or any white fish for this recipe. This is
a really simple recipe and the fingers can be made in
minutes. Polenta flour is really versatile and makes a
fantastic crispy coating.*

• Thoroughly grease and line a baking tray, as the
batter will stick to it.

• Mix the batter ingredients in a bowl, along with
210ml water. Dip in the fish pieces, making sure they
are evenly coated in the batter.

• Place on the high rack and cook at 200°C for 15–20
minutes until cooked through and golden.

Vegetarian

You don't have to be a vegetarian to enjoy these delicious dishes. It is extremely good for your health to have meat-free days, as you consume less saturated fat. Add a wide variety of coloured vegetables to your diet. This enhances your phytonutrients, including antioxidants. Also add pulses, beans and wholegrains. You will find recipes in this chapter using Quorn, a vegetarian alternative to meat, which contains up to 80 per cent less saturated fat.

Chilli, ginger and lime-stuffed squash

1–2 butternut
squash
Chilli oil
50g quinoa
50g brown rice
$1/2$ tsp coconut oil
or olive oil
1 large red onion,
peeled and diced
2–4 cloves of garlic,
peeled and
roughly
chopped/crushed
1–2 chillies (to
taste), finely
chopped
1cm piece of
ginger, peeled
and finely grated
1–2 red peppers,
finely chopped
Small handful of
spring onions,
finely chopped
6 cherry tomatoes,
quartered
Juice and zest of
$1/2$ lime
Small handful of
chopped
coriander
Salad, to serve

This is a really tasty dish. Even if you don't fancy the idea of eating squash, give this a go, as you will be pleasantly surprised. I love chillies, so this packs a bit of a kick, but you can cut down on the chillies or cut them out completely if you prefer.

• Cut the squash in half and remove the seeds. Brush the insides with chilli oil. Place on the high rack at 190°C and cook for 15 minutes.

• Meanwhile, rinse the quinoa and place it in a saucepan with water. The best way to measure the quantity of water needed is to put the quinoa in a cup. You will need $1^1/2$ times the amount of water to quinoa. Boil for 15 minutes.

• Do the same with the brown rice.

• Meanwhile, place the oil in a sauté pan and add the onion, garlic, chillies, ginger, red peppers and spring onions. Cook until they are just starting to soften. Remove from heat.

• Drain the cooked rice and quinoa and add to the onion mixture. Stir in the remaining ingredients.

• Remove the squash from the halogen and fill both halves with the mixture. Drizzle over a little more chilli oil if you like more of a kick. Wrap the squash in foil as this stops it from drying out.

• Return to the oven and cook for a further 10 minutes.

• Serve immediately with salad.

Healthy tip! *Squash is packed with antioxidants. Quinoa is packed full of protein and fibre so helps keep you fuller for longer.*

Roasted vegetable curry

I adore curries and roasted vegetables, so why not put the two together? It creates a very simple curry dish that tastes fantastic.

• Preheat the halogen oven to 220°C or use the preheat setting.

• Place the onions, potatoes, butternut squash and carrots in an ovenproof dish. Drizzle with olive oil and a sprinkle of paprika, and season to taste. Toss until combined, ensuring the vegetables are evenly coated.

• Place the vegetables on the high rack and cook for 20 minutes.

• Meanwhile, place the coriander seeds and cumin seeds in a sauté pan and dry fry for 1–2 minutes. When the fragrance starts to break through, remove from the heat and grind with a pestle and mortar.

• In a liquidiser, add the turmeric, garam masala, chilli, garlic, ginger, coriander and seasoning. Whiz and add enough olive oil (about 2–3 tablespoons) to form a liquid paste.

• Heat the paste in the sauté pan. Add 300ml of water and combine while bringing up to the boil, then turn off the heat. Stir the coconut milk and Greek yoghurt into the pan and set aside.

• When the 20-minute timer beeps, add the peppers and tomatoes to the dish and return to the oven for a further 15 minutes. Add a drizzle more oil if necessary.

• Remove the vegetables from the oven. Add these to the paste in the sauté pan. Add more water if you want a more liquid curry, bearing in mind that some will evaporate during the cooking. Cook for 5–10 minutes until the vegetables are cooked to your liking.

• Sprinkle with coriander leaves. Serve with fluffy, fragrant rice, yoghurt and chutney.

2 red onions, peeled and cut into wedges
1–2 sweet potatoes, peeled and thickly diced
1 potato, thickly diced
$1/2$ or 1 small butternut squash, cut into 2cm thick chunks or wedges (no need to peel)
1–2 carrots, peeled and thickly sliced
Olive oil
Paprika
Salt and freshly ground black pepper
1 tsp coriander seeds
1 tsp cumin seeds
2 tsp turmeric
2–3 tsp garam masala
1 red chilli
4 cloves garlic, peeled
2.5cm piece of ginger, peeled
Small handful of coriander leaves
150–200ml low-fat coconut milk
3 tbsp Greek yoghurt
1 red pepper, thickly sliced
1 yellow pepper, thickly sliced
3–4 tomatoes, cut into wedges
Fragrant rice, yoghurt and chutney, to serve

Potato, cheese and vegetable frittata

5 eggs, beaten
1 bunch of spring
onions, finely
chopped
1 red pepper, diced
2–3 tomatoes,
roughly chopped
300g cooked
potatoes, sliced
or cubed
50–75g low-fat
mature Cheddar,
grated
1 tsp thyme
(optional)
Salt and freshly
ground black
pepper
Salad, to serve

This is an ideal dish for using up any leftover cooked potatoes and vegetables. Anything goes, so feel free to adapt this recipe.

• Preheat the halogen oven to 200°C or use the preheat setting.

• In a large bowl, break the eggs and beat well. Add the remaining ingredients and combine.

• Pour into a well-greased ovenproof dish.

• Place on the low rack and cook for 20–25 minutes until firm.

• Serve hot or cold with a salad.

Did you know? *Eggs are packed full of key nutrients, but in particular protein. They also contain choline, which can help metabolise fats and has even been shown to improve memory.*

Courgette, Parmesan and chilli patties

These patties are gorgeous – perfect for a lovely supper on a summer's evening. I serve them with a selection of dips, new potato salad and green salad – or for a quick snack, just a sweet chilli dip!

• Heat a little oil in a sauté pan and fry the garlic, spring onions and chillies for 2–3 minutes before adding the courgettes. Cook until soft, then remove from heat.

• In a bowl, mix the eggs, crème fraîche and Parmesan together. Season to taste and stir in the courgette mixture.

• Form into four large or eight small patties and place on a well-greased baking tray.

• Preheat the halogen oven to 200°C or use the preheat setting.

• Place the tray on the high rack and cook the patties for 20–25 minutes until golden.

• Serve with a salad or on their own with sweet chilli sauce.

Olive oil
2–3 cloves of garlic, peeled and crushed
Small bunch of spring onions, finely sliced
1–2 chillies (to taste), finely sliced
4–5 courgettes, grated
3 eggs
75g low-fat crème fraîche
40g grated Parmesan cheese
Salt and freshly ground black pepper
Salad or sweet chilli sauce, to serve

Serves

4

Olive oil

1 red onion, peeled and finely chopped

1–3 cloves of garlic (to taste), peeled and crushed

1 red pepper, diced

300g Quorn mince

50g white or chestnut mushrooms, chopped

400g can chopped tomatoes

2 tbsp sun-dried tomato purée

200ml low-calorie red wine

Salt and freshly ground black pepper

1 tsp dried oregano

Few basil leaves (optional)

8 extra-large beef tomatoes

Salad, to serve

Quorn bolognaise-stuffed tomatoes

Perfect for using up any leftover bolognaise, or why not double up the bolognaise recipe and make two dishes?

• Heat a spray of olive oil in a sauté pan and cook the onion, garlic and red pepper until they start to soften.

• Add the Quorn and cook for 5 minutes, then add the mushrooms, tomatoes, tomato purée and wine.

• Season to taste and add the oregano and basil.

• Simmer for 10 minutes. Add a little water if the sauce looks too dry.

• Cut the tops off the beef tomatoes, setting them aside to use as lids. Scoop out the centre of the tomatoes (you can chop these up and add them to the bolognaise). You will be left with a tomato shell.

• When the bolognaise is cooked, fill the tomatoes but don't overfill them. Place the lids on top and put the tomatoes on a baking tray.

• Spray with olive oil and season.

• Place on the low rack and bake at 200°C for 15–20 minutes.

• Serve immediately with a lovely salad.

Healthy cottage pie

I really hope non-vegetarians read this chapter! This recipe oozes with goodness: packed with fabulous pulses and beans, which not only help lower cholesterol and maintain great digestive health, but also keep you fuller for longer. Add to this all the antioxidant-rich vegetables used here and you can see where this recipe gets its name from.

• Make sure the potatoes, swede and carrot are cut into equal-size chunks. Place into a steamer and cook until soft. This should take about 20 minutes.

• Meanwhile, heat the oil in a sauté pan on a medium heat.

• Add the onion, garlic, red pepper, celery and carrots, and cook gently for 5–10 minutes until they start to soften.

• Add the lentils, beans and tomatoes. Fill the empty tomato can halfway with water and add this to the mixture. Add the Worcestershire sauce, parsley, paprika and yeast extract. Simmer gently and add more liquid if necessary.

• Check the steamed vegetables. If they are done, mash them with the milk. Season to taste with black pepper.

• Place the lentil and bean mixture in an ovenproof dish. Spoon over the mash and sprinkle with the cheese.

• Place on the low rack and cook at 200°C for 20 minutes.

• Serve with steamed green vegetables.

2 sweet potatoes, peeled and chopped

2–3 large potatoes, peeled and chopped

$1/4$ swede, peeled and chopped

1 large carrot, peeled and chopped

1 tsp coconut oil or olive oil

1 red onion, peeled and finely chopped

2 cloves of garlic, peeled and finely chopped

1 red pepper, finely diced

2 sticks of celery, finely diced

2 carrots, peeled and finely diced

400g can brown lentils, drained

400g can borlotti beans, drained

400g can chopped tomatoes

3–4 splashes of Worcestershire sauce (if strict vegetarian, use a vegetarian version)

1 tsp dried parsley

1 tsp paprika

1 tsp yeast extract

100ml skimmed milk

30g low-fat mature Cheddar, grated

Steamed green vegetables, to serve

Courgette, spinach and ricotta spaghetti

2–3 courgettes, thickly sliced

1 onion, peeled and finely chopped

2 cloves of garlic, peeled and roughly chopped

1–2 tsp coconut oil or olive oil

Salt and freshly ground black pepper

300g wholemeal spaghetti

100g baby leaf spinach

150g low-fat ricotta cheese

50ml skimmed milk

1–2 tbsp freshly grated Parmesan cheese (optional)

This is a great dish to make if you're in a hurry. Use wholemeal spaghetti and it makes a filling meal.

• Place the courgettes, onion and garlic in an ovenproof dish. Drizzle with a little oil and season to taste.

• Place on the high rack and cook at 210°C for 15 minutes until soft.

• Meanwhile, cook the spaghetti following packet instructions.

• While the pasta is cooking, wilt the spinach by placing it in a bowl and pouring over boiling water. Leave for 2 minutes. Drain and mix with the ricotta and milk.

• When the pasta is cooked, drain and tip back into the saucepan over a low heat. Add the ricotta mixture and stir well. Stir in the cooked courgettes and onion.

• Season with black pepper and sprinkle with Parmesan, if using. Serve immediately.

Did you know? *Spinach is a rich source of the B vitamin folic acid. Studies have shown spinach can help protect against heart disease by lowering homocysteine levels. Other sources of folate include broccoli, lentils, avocado and asparagus.*

Tofu and vegetable kebabs

I love tofu but it does need to absorb flavours otherwise it can be very bland. I leave it to marinate in a few teaspoons of soy sauce for at least 1 hour before making this dish.

• If you are using wooden skewers, soak them in water overnight.

• Marinate the tofu in the soy sauce for at least 1 hour.

• Chop the vegetables into equal-size chunks.

• Thread the vegetables, tofu chunks and bay leaves onto four skewers.

• Brush the tofu with sweet chilli sauce.

• Place on the high rack and grill at 250°C, turning regularly and brushing with more chilli sauce.

• Serve on a bed of brown or basmati rice.

350–400g firm tofu, cut into chunks
2 tsp soy sauce
1 red onion, peeled
1 green, yellow, red or orange pepper
1 courgette
Handful of bay leaves
Sweet chilli sauce
Brown or basmati rice, to serve

Did you know? *Tofu is made from soya beans. It is a great source of phytonutrients, being shown to aid in balancing hormones, particularly in women experiencing the menopause. It is also an excellent source of protein, so great for vegetarians/vegans or those wanting to avoid eating too much red meat. It has also been shown to help lower cholesterol. Tofu is quite bland on its own but does absorb the flavours around it really well.*

Butternut squash risotto

1–2 tsp coconut oil
or olive oil

1 onion, peeled and
finely chopped

2 cloves of garlic,
peeled and
crushed

400g Arborio risotto
rice

800g butternut
squash, peeled
and diced

1.25 litres hot
vegetable stock

2 tbsp Greek
yoghurt

30g Parmesan
cheese, finely
grated

Freshly ground
black pepper

This is an easy way of making risotto and saves you slaving over a hot stove! You can sauté the onions and garlic in the halogen but I find it much easier to start this dish on the hob and then transfer to an ovenproof dish ready to pop in the halogen oven.

• Heat the oil in a sauté pan. Add the onion and garlic and cook until the onion starts to soften.

• Stir in the rice and butternut squash. Pour in the stock and bring up to the boil.

• Transfer to an ovenproof dish and cover securely with a layer of foil.

• Place on the low rack and cook at 180°C for 30 minutes.

• Remove and stir in the yoghurt, Parmesan and black pepper to taste.

• Return to the oven for a further 5 minutes before serving.

Sun-dried tomato, pepper, red onion and pesto frittata

This is lovely hot or cold. Cut into wedges and enjoy with a salad.

• Add the oil to a deep 20cm round ovenproof dish. Place on the high rack and heat at 230°C for 1 minute.

• Add the red onions and red peppers. Cook for 5 minutes until the vegetables start to soften.

• Meanwhile, beat the eggs, yoghurt and flour together in a bowl. Season with black pepper.

• Carefully pour the egg mixture into the dish. Add the sun-dried tomatoes and pesto evenly over the egg mixture.

• Cook for 5 minutes, then turn the temperature down to 190°C and cook for a further 15–20 minutes until the egg is firm to the touch and golden on top.

• Serve hot or cold.

ADD! If you are a cheese addict, you could add some crumbled goat's cheese, or low-fat feta to the dish at the same time as the sun-dried tomatoes and pesto, but remember that it will add more salt and fat to the dish.

1 tsp coconut oil or olive oil
1 large or 2 small red onions, peeled and finely sliced
1–2 red peppers, finely sliced
4 eggs
200g Greek yoghurt
3 tbsp plain flour
Freshly ground black pepper
6–8 sun-dried tomatoes, drained of oil
4 tsp red or green pesto

Did you know? Eggs are a rich source of selenium, iron and B vitamins.

Tomato, garlic, goat's cheese and rocket pizza

12 cherry tomatoes,
    halved
2 cloves of garlic,
    peeled and
    roughly chopped
Freshly ground
    black pepper
2 tbsp olive oil
1 tbsp balsamic
    vinegar
1 sprig of thyme
1 wholemeal
    floured tortilla
80g goat's cheese
50g rocket

This pizza uses a wholemeal tortilla base so is not only simple to prepare but also lighter on fat and calories.

• Place the tomatoes in an ovenproof dish. Sprinkle with the garlic and season with black pepper.

• In a small bowl, mix the olive oil and balsamic vinegar together. Sprinkle half onto the tomatoes and leave the rest to one side. Add the thyme to the tomatoes.

• Place on the high rack and cook at 210°C for 10 minutes.

• Place the floured tortilla on a greased ovenproof dish. Sprinkle over the crumbled goat's cheese.

• Remove the tomatoes from the oven and distribute evenly over the tortilla.

• Return to the oven and cook for a further 10 minutes.

• Sprinkle with the rocket and finish with a drizzle of the olive oil/vinegar mixture before serving.

Spiced chickpea and tofu burgers

You don't have to be vegetarian to enjoy these tasty burgers. Serve in a wholemeal bap or pitta, or roll the mixture into small balls and serve in a wrap with some crunchy salad. Delicious hot or cold.

• Heat ¹/₂ teaspoon of the oil in a sauté pan. Add the onion, garlic and celery and cook until they start to soften. Remove from heat.

• In a food processor, whiz the tofu and chickpeas together with the chilli, spices and herbs.

• Transfer to a bowl and stir in the cooked onion, garlic and celery.

• Add the grated carrot and combine well. Season to taste before forming into balls and pressing into four to six burger patties.

• Place on greaseproof paper. The patties can be stored in the fridge or frozen until needed.

• Place the burgers directly on the high rack (or grill rack if you have one) and grill at 235°C or higher if your machine allows, for 6–8 minutes on each side (a little less if they are smaller), turning regularly to ensure they cook evenly.

1 tsp coconut oil or olive oil
1 large onion, peeled and finely chopped
2 cloves of garlic, peeled and crushed
1 stick of celery, finely diced
350–400g tofu, drained
400g can chickpeas, drained
1 chilli
1 tsp ground cumin
1 tsp paprika
1 tsp ground coriander
2 tbsp fresh coriander
1 tbsp fresh parsley
1 carrot, peeled and grated
Salt and freshly ground black pepper

Skinny macaroni cheese

250g wholemeal
macaroni
1 tsp butter or low-
fat spread (or 2
tsp if you're not
using coconut
oil)
1 tsp coconut oil
1 heaped tbsp
wholemeal plain
flour
500–700ml
skimmed milk
1–2 tbsp nutritional
yeast flakes
(optional)
1 tsp yellow or
wholegrain
mustard
(optional)
80g low-fat mature
Cheddar or
Parmesan
cheese, grated
Freshly ground
black pepper
50g oats
75g wholemeal
breadcrumbs
25g mixed seeds

Macaroni cheese is a great comfort supper but with white macaroni, full-fat cheese and full-fat milk it can be a dieter's downfall. This is a simple tweak on the traditional recipe. Nutritional yeast flakes can give a great cheese flavour, plus added B vitamins. You do need to use wholemeal pasta rather than white. You can make a sauce by melting low-fat cream cheese with a little milk but I find it lacks substance, so this recipe is made using a traditional white sauce.

• Place the macaroni in a pan of boiling water and cook following packet instructions.

• Meanwhile, make the sauce. In a saucepan, heat the butter or low-fat spread and oil over a medium heat. Add the flour and blend, using a wooden spoon, to form a paste.

• Very gradually add the milk, stirring continually to form a lump-free sauce. If the sauce becomes lumpy, use a balloon whisk and beat well.

• When you have a smooth sauce, start adding the flavours. Stir in the nutritional yeast flakes and mustard (if using) and cheese, and season with black pepper. Taste as you go to ensure you get the right flavour. Make sure the sauce isn't too thick as it will thicken further when added to the pasta.

• Drain the macaroni and add it to the sauce, stirring well. Tip into an ovenproof dish.

• In a bowl, mix the oats, breadcrumbs and seeds together. Sprinkle over the macaroni.

• Place on the low rack. If the sauce and macaroni are still warm you will only need to brown off the top for 10 minutes at 200°C. If you have prepared this in advance, it will need to cook for 20 minutes.

• Serve piping hot!

Roasted vegetable ratatouille

Simple yet totally delicious! Just chop and go!

• Combine all the vegetables in an ovenproof dish. Pour over a drizzle of olive oil, a dash of balsamic vinegar and a sprinkle of salt and sugar. Add the herb sprigs and toss again.

• Place on the high rack and cook at 200°C for 40 minutes.

• Stir in the passata and season with black pepper. Return to the oven and cook for a further 15 minutes.

• Serve with crusty bread.

ADD! For added yumminess, add some cubed feta cheese before serving.

Did you know? *Vitamin A is found in orange-coloured vegetables and fruit, such as carrots, squash, orange and red peppers, mangoes, apricots and peaches, as well as liver and oily fish.*

---

2 red peppers, cut into thick wedges
2 red onions, peeled and cut into wedges
4–5 cloves of garlic, peeled and halved
8–10 tomatoes, scored but left whole
1 small aubergine, cut into thick wedges
2 courgettes, cut into lengthways wedges
Olive oil
Balsamic vinegar
Salt and freshly ground black pepper
Sugar
Fresh thyme and rosemary sprigs
500ml jar of passata
Crusty bread, to serve

Falafels

2 x 400g cans
    chickpeas, rinsed
    and drained
3–4 cloves of garlic,
    peeled and
    crushed
1 small onion,
    peeled
2 tbsp tahini paste
1 egg
1–2 tsp ground
    cumin
1 tsp ground
    coriander
$1/2$ tsp chilli powder
Squeeze of lemon
    juice
3–4 tbsp
    breadcrumbs
Salad or pitta
    pockets, to serve

I love these falafels! They are so easy to make and taste delicious with a lovely selection of salad leaves. Perfect alfresco food.

• Place all the ingredients, apart from the breadcrumbs, in a food processor and whiz to a moist paste.

• Scrape into a bowl and cover with clingfilm. Leave in the fridge for at least 2 hours to allow the flavours to develop.

• When ready to make, tip the breadcrumbs onto a plate. Scoop enough of the mixture to form it into a 2–3cm ball – you may need to flour your hands first. Repeat until all the mixture has been used.

• Roll the balls in the breadcrumbs, ensuring they are properly coated. Place the balls on a greased non-stick baking tray.

• Place on the high rack and cook at 200°C for 15–20 minutes, turning occasionally to ensure they are cooked and browned all over.

• Serve hot or cold with salad, or stuffed into pitta pockets.

Roast vegetable frittata

If I am making roasted vegetables to accompany another dish, I double the quantities and either make this or a roasted vegetable ratatouille. I love the flavours of roasted vegetables but you can add a little more pizazz by adding some fresh herbs, chopped chillies, or for non-vegetarians, some chorizo or bacon. You can use any vegetables you may have in the fridge, but these are my favourites.

• Put the oil in a roasting tin. Place on the high rack and heat at 200°C for 2 minutes.

• Add the vegetables to the oil, tossing until evenly coated. Add the thyme or rosemary.

• Return to the high rack and cook for 25–40 minutes until the vegetables are soft and roasted.

• Meanwhile, mix the eggs with the milk and season to taste with black pepper. When the vegetables are cooked, pour the egg mixture onto the vegetables while they are still in the oven.

• Cook for a further 20–25 minutes until the frittata has puffed up and is golden on top.

• Serve with a green salad.

2 tsp coconut oil or olive oil

2 red onions, peeled and cut into wedges

2–3 cloves of garlic, peeled and roughly chopped

2 peppers, cut into thick slices

2 sweet potatoes, peeled and cut into thick chunks

1 courgette, cut into thick chunks

8 cherry tomatoes, left whole

2–3 sprigs of fresh thyme or rosemary

6 eggs, beaten

150ml skimmed milk

Freshly ground black pepper

Green salad, to serve

Mediterranean-style pasta bake

300g wholemeal
  penne
1 tsp coconut oil or
  olive oil
1 red onion, peeled
  and finely
  chopped
2 cloves of garlic,
  peeled and
  roughly chopped
2 courgettes, sliced
1 red pepper, diced
400g can chopped
  tomatoes
1–2 sprigs of thyme
Salt and freshly
  ground black
  pepper
Red wine (optional)
30g Parmesan
  cheese, grated
Salad, to serve

Pasta is a quick and easy meal but using white pasta adds unwanted pounds. Swap for a wholemeal or vegetable pasta for a more nutrient-rich, wholesome dish.

• Place the dried pasta in a pan of boiling water and cook following packet instructions.

• Meanwhile, heat the oil in a sauté pan and add the onion, garlic, courgettes and red pepper. Cook until they start to soften, then add the tomatoes and thyme. Season to taste. If you like a richer sauce you might want to add a glug or two of red wine.

• Drain the pasta and add it to the vegetable mixture. Combine well before transferring to an ovenproof dish. Sprinkle with the Parmesan.

• Place on the medium rack and cook at 220°C for about 5 minutes until golden and bubbling.

• Serve immediately with a selection of salad leaves.

Roasted vegetable mushroom pizzas

Serves

4

Pizza dough can be quite calorific and carb-rich, so this recipe uses large mushrooms as a base. You can fill them with your own choice of vegetables and toppings but this is a family favourite of ours.

- Place the oil in an ovenproof dish. Add the onion, red pepper, courgette and tomatoes.

- Place on the high rack and cook at 210°C for 15 minutes.

- Brush the mushrooms with garlic-infused olive oil. Add them to the roasted vegetables and cook for a further 5 minutes.

- Remove the vegetables and mushrooms from the oven.

- Spread the tomato purée inside the mushrooms, then fill with the roasted vegetables.

- Top with the crumbled feta or goat's cheese.

- Return to the oven and cook for 10 minutes until golden and bubbling.

- Serve with a selection of salad leaves.

Did you know? *According to the World Health Organisation (WHO), 65 per cent of the world's population now lives in countries where being overweight and obese kill more people than being underweight.*

---

1 tsp coconut oil or olive oil
1 large red onion, peeled and sliced
1 red pepper, sliced
1 courgette, sliced
6 cherry or vine tomatoes, halved
4 large Portobello mushrooms
Garlic-infused olive oil
2 tbsp sun-dried tomato purée
80g feta or goat's cheese, crumbled
Salad, to serve

Lentil dahl

Olive oil

1 red onion, peeled and chopped

2 cloves of garlic, peeled and crushed

1 green, yellow, red or orange pepper, chopped (optional)

2.5–5cm piece of fresh ginger, peeled and chopped

2 tbsp mild or sweet curry powder

1–2 tsp turmeric

1–2 tomatoes, finely chopped

100g red lentils

Chopped coriander or desiccated coconut, to serve

Lentils are high in magnesium, low in fat and a good protein source. This dish is so easy to make and costs very little. You can make it mild and creamy by adding some fat-free Greek yoghurt – ideal for children – or spice it up to suit your taste.

• Heat the oil in a large pan. Fry the onion, garlic, pepper and ginger until soft.

• Add the curry powder, turmeric and tomatoes, and cook for a further 2 minutes.

• Transfer to an ovenproof dish. Add the lentils and cover with 300ml boiling water.

• Cover with a double layer of foil (or a lid if you have one).

• Place on the low rack and cook at 190°C for 30–40 minutes.

• Add up to 100ml more boiling water if necessary. The lentils should be soft and in a lovely thick sauce.

• Sprinkle with the chopped herbs or coconut before serving.

Did you know? *Lentils are packed full of fibre and are also a great source of magnesium. They are known to help balance blood-sugar levels.*

Quorn meatball hotpot

This is one of my son's favourite dishes. You can use lean meatballs but Quorn is low in fat and tastes so good. Quorn is lower in saturated fat than minced meat so this is a great replacement for meat eaters.

• Cut the potatoes into quarters. Place them in a pan to steam or boil (steaming is healthier).

• Meanwhile, spray a little olive oil in a sauté pan and heat. Add the onion, garlic and red pepper and cook until they start to soften.

• Add the tomatoes. Fill the tomato can almost full of water and add this to the sauté pan. Add the thyme, black pepper and meatballs. Simmer gently for 10 minutes.

• When the potatoes are almost cooked, remove them from the pan.

• Layer half the potatoes in a casserole dish. Add the meatball mixture and top with the remaining potatoes.

• Season and cover with the cheese.

• Place on the low rack and bake at 190°C for 15 minutes until golden.

• Serve immediately.

Did you know? *Onions and garlic contain allicin, which helps fight disease and can help lower blood pressure.*

1kg new potatoes
Olive oil
1 red onion, peeled and sliced
2 cloves of garlic, peeled and crushed
1 red pepper, diced
400g can chopped tomatoes
1 tbsp fresh thyme, chopped
Salt and freshly ground black pepper
300g pack of Quorn meatballs
50g low-fat mature Cheddar cheese

Vegetable and butterbean crumble

1 red onion, peeled
and finely
chopped

2–3 cloves of garlic,
peeled and
roughly chopped

1 red pepper, sliced

1 green pepper,
sliced

2 courgettes, sliced

1/2 aubergine, diced

1 sweet potato,
peeled and diced

Spray of olive oil

2–3 sprigs of thyme

400g can chopped
tomatoes

400g can
butterbeans,
drained

150ml hot water or
low-salt
vegetable stock

Salt and freshly
ground black
pepper

Salad, to serve

For the crumble

75g wholemeal
flour

25g regular or low-
fat margarine

40g oats

30g wholemeal
breadcrumbs

25g chopped
peanuts

25g sunflower
seeds

25g pumpkin seed

2 tbsp linseeds

*This can be prepared in advance and even frozen
uncooked, ready to cook when needed.*

• Place the vegetables on a baking tray. Spray with a
little olive oil and add the thyme.

• Place on the high rack and bake at 190°C for 20
minutes.

• Meanwhile, prepare the crumble. Rub the flour with
the margarine to form breadcrumbs.

• Mix in the remaining ingredients, season to taste and
set aside.

• Remove the roasted vegetables from the oven. Place
in an ovenproof dish, and stir in the tomatoes,
butterbeans and water or stock. Season to taste.

• Cover with the crumble mix.

• Return to the oven on the low rack, turn the
temperature down to 180°C and cook for 15–20
minutes.

• Serve with a salad.

Did you know? *Peanuts are a good source of vitamin E,
which is also found in almonds, sunflower seeds, hazelnuts
and seed oils.*

Sweet Treats

We all love a treat but when we are following a healthy diet we avoid
these like the plague, which only makes our craving stronger. The
recipes in this chapter are kinder to our bodies and health, though
that doesn't mean you can binge! Everything in moderation.

Cake baking and the halogen

You can bake cakes, biscuits and treats in a halogen oven. There are a few tips to help, so give it a go with your favourite recipe and see how you get on. Since publishing previous books on cooking with a halogen oven, I have had lots of emails from readers. One thing that seems to keep cropping up is fluctuations in temperature for different machines. The paragraphs below address this, so read on.

Read!

Always read the recipe right through before you start. Not only does this help you to familiarise yourself with what you have to do, but it also gives you time to check your ingredients and equipment, and work out timings. There is no point starting a recipe and getting halfway through only to find you have to soak something overnight before proceeding to the next step, or that you're missing a vital ingredient!

Preparing the cake tins

I can't emphasise enough the importance of lining/greasing cake tins before baking. I am a recent convert to cake tin liners. You can buy them from your local supermarket and they are well worth the investment. You can also buy reusable baking sheets which are great, but remember that most will be made to fit conventional ovens, so you will have to make adjustments or seek alternatives for your halogen.

Cake-making tips

You may follow a recipe to the letter but your cake decides not to come out exactly as the celebrity chef's. Why is that? With cake baking so many factors can affect the end result: temperature variations in halogens is just one of them (there has been lots of feedback stating some machines can be as much as 30°C out!). Here are some basic tips to help:
- A doughy cake is often caused by too little rising agent, unsifted flour or not baking for long enough or at the right temperature for the cake to rise.
- A heavy cake can be caused by not mixing (adding enough air to the mixture) correctly, not sifting the flour, not using enough rising agent or too much flour.
- A dry cake tends to be overcooked, so if this keeps happening, check your timings. Or maybe the mixture didn't have enough butter or wet ingredients in it. If your fruitcakes are dry, try adding a grated carrot or apple, or even a mashed banana to the mixture to help moisten the cake.
- Fruit that sinks to the bottom of the cake is mainly due to adding the fruit too soon (i.e. cream butter and sugar, add beaten eggs, then sifted flour, before adding the fruit). You may not have combined the fruit well enough,

or simply made the cake mixture too thin, so it could not hold the additional ingredients.

- Sunken cakes are normally caused by those impatient souls who can't resist opening the oven door every few minutes 'just to check' – that's what glass doors are for! Your cake mixture may also be too wet.
- If the top is burnt but the middle uncooked, the oven temperature is too hot. Turn the temperature down a little and cook for longer. Some say that covering a cake with foil helps it cook faster – don't follow this advice as you won't get the right results. Remember, you can't rush perfection!
- A cracked top is due to the oven being too hot. Turn the temperature down and cook for a little longer.
- An uneven surface (one side risen and the other sunken) can indicate uneven temperature.
- Preheat the oven. I know the halogen appears not to require this, but old habits die hard and I prefer to preheat and know that when my cake goes in the oven it starts cooking immediately.

When things go wrong

Don't panic if things go wrong – it happens. When I learnt to cook at school, we were told to weigh eggs, always use butter and only self-raising or plain flour. Now we never weigh eggs, which can cause a mixture to be too wet or too dry. Flour quality varies so much: I recently started using high-grade sponge flour, which makes very light cakes, but the mixture is wetter and in some cases I have had to increase the flour quantity for the recipe. Cheap margarine can throw a cake mixture; some are better than others so make sure you use good-quality margarine. I use Stork or butter.

Temperature fluctuations

- When using the halogen remember that temperature fluctuations can occur. If you suspect this, test the temperature with an oven thermometer. I would advise baking simple fairy cakes, which take 12–15 minutes in the halogen, to gauge how your machine works. It will also give you confidence to progress on to other cakes.
- If the cake is too near the element it will burn on the top, so either use an extension ring or place it on the low rack.
- If the cake seems to be cooking quickly on top but the middle and bottom are still raw, reduce the temperature and cook for longer. I often cook larger cakes for 60+ minutes, especially fruitcakes or apple cake.
- Always test the cake to see if it is cooked before you turn it out – there is nothing more upsetting than turning out a cake and finding the bottom isn't cooked.

Sugar

You will see that the use of sugar is limited in this book. Instead I opt for natural sweetners such as xylitol or stevia (see p. 11). The good news is these sweetners do not heave the negative effects of sugar (or artificial sweeteners), so you can enjoy them guilt-free. Xylitol can be used as a direct replacement for sugar, so for ease of use I have used this in the recipes. If you want to use stevia, then be aware that you need a lot less as it is very sweet. You will need to adjust the quantity to taste or as directed by the manufacturer.

Spicy apple and sultana cake

These quantities make a small loaf cake. If you want a larger cake, double up the quantities. Remember, you will have to cook larger cakes for longer.

SUITABLE FOR GLUTEN FREE DIETS AND SUGAR-FREE DIETS

• Preheat the halogen oven to 180°C.

• Mix the oil, yoghurt and egg together in a jug.

• Place all the dry ingredients in a bowl and combine well before adding the egg mixture. Fold in the apples and sultanas until well combined.

• Pour the mixture into a greased and lined 1lb loaf tin.

• Place on the low rack and bake for 20 minutes, then reduce the temperature to 160°C and cook for a further 15–20 minutes. To test if the cake is done, insert a skewer or the tip of a sharp knife in the centre of the cake. If it comes out clean, it is cooked; if it comes out wet, it needs a little longer. Check every 5–10 minutes.

• Turn out onto a cooling rack before serving.

Did you know? *Oats are a great source of fibre. They also help lower cholesterol and help balance blood-sugar levels.*

75ml light olive oil or rapeseed oil

80ml fat-free Greek yoghurt

1 egg

140g wholemeal flour (or Doves Farm gluten-free flour) (add 30ml milk if using gluten-free flour)

1 tsp baking powder (or gluten-free baking powder)

90g oats (or gluten-free oats)

30g oat bran (or gluten-free oat bran)

60g xylitol

1 tsp cinnamon

$1/2$ tsp ground coriander

$1/4$ tsp mixed spice

1–2 cooking apples, peeled and chopped

40g sultanas

50g dried
cranberries, finely
chopped

150g dried apricots,
finely chopped

75ml orange juice

4 tbsp agave syrup

2 tbsp coconut oil

1–2 tsp pure vanilla
extract

2 tbsp apple purée
(or stewed
apple/unsweetened
apple sauce)

120g porridge oats

6 plain rice cakes,
crumbled

25g mixed seeds

50g brown sugar

On-the-go flapjacks

These flapjacks contain a bit of everything, giving you a delicious, filling snack when you are on the move. You can drizzle dark chocolate over the top for extra decadence, but do make sure it is at least 70% cocoa solids. For an extra chocolatey hit, add a handful of dark chocolate chips to the mixture before baking.

• Place the dried fruit in a bowl and pour over the orange juice. Leave to soak for at least 1 hour.

• Place the agave syrup, oil and vanilla in a saucepan. Heat very gently until runny, then remove from heat. Stir in the apple purée.

• In a large bowl, add the porridge oats, rice cakes, seeds and sugar. Pour over the syrup mixture and add the dried fruit. Combine well.

• Pour the mixture into a greased and lined 16–18cm tin.

• Place on the low rack and cook at 190°C for 20 minutes.

• Remove from the oven and cut into slices.

• Store in an airtight container for up to four days.

Did you know? *Cranberries are a great source of the flavonoid anthocyanin – a powerful antioxidant that can help prevent free-radical damage, has anti-inflammatory properties and also a unique ability to combat urinary problems such as cystitis (though you are better off treating cystitis by taking concentrated cranberry powder).*

Goji and orange flapjacks

I love these flapjacks. They're perfect to have in a tin when you're feeling peckish or for packed lunches. If you're a bit dubious about goji berries, replace them with dried cranberries.

• Soak the goji berries in the orange juice for at least 1 hour.

• Mix the remaining ingredients together, along with the berries and the juice, in a bowl, combining well.

• Pour the mixture into a greased and lined 16–18cm baking dish. Level the surface with the back of a spoon.

• Place on the low rack and bake at 190°C for 20–30 minutes until firm and golden.

• Remove from the oven and cut into slices.

• Store in an airtight container for up to four days.

Did you know? Oats are a fantastic source of fibre, help lower cholesterol and can help balance blood-sugar levels. They keep you fuller for longer, so are the perfect choice when you are watching your weight.

100g goji berries
200ml orange juice
Zest of 1 orange
3 heaped tbsp apple
    purée (or stewed
    apple/unsweetened
    apple sauce)
250g oats
30g mixed seeds
50g xylitol
2 tbsp agave syrup
1–2 tsp ground
    cinnamon

Apple, date and cinnamon breakfast muffins

175g wholemeal or granary flour
30g xylitol or brown sugar
175g coarse polenta
1 tbsp baking powder
1 egg, beaten
280ml buttermilk
2 cooking apples (I use Bramley), peeled and diced
6–8 dates, diced
2–3 tsp ground cinnamon

If you don't have time for breakfast, grab one of these muffins – they are perfect for a mid-morning snack. You will need silicon muffin cases to make these. Grease the muffin cases and place them on a baking tray before filling with the mixture. If you are using small cases, halve the quantities. Suitable for freezing.

• Place the dry ingredients in a bowl and combine well.

• In a jug, mix the egg with the buttermilk, then pour into the dry ingredients and combine well.

• Stir in the apples, dates and cinnamon.

• Fill the silicon muffin cases to three-quarters.

• Place the tray on the low rack and bake at 200°C for 12–20 minutes (cooking times depend on the size of the cases used). To test if the muffins are done, press the top gently with a finger. If the sponge springs back, they are ready.

• Serve hot or cold. Store in an airtight container for up to four days.

Lemon and poppy-seed cake

This is one of my favourite cakes. I make it in a single sponge tin and it is delicious hot or cold. I love lemons, so I tend to add quite a lot of zest! If you like the lemon drizzle effect, I have explained how to do this at the end of the recipe.

SUITABLE FOR GLUTEN-FREE DIETS

• In a bowl, mix the butter and xylitol/sugar together until creamy. Add the eggs one at a time. If the mixture looks like it will curdle, add a little of the polenta flour.

• Add the polenta flour and ground almonds, and stir in the baking powder. Combine well.

• Add the lemon zest and lemon extract, if using, for extra zing!

• Stir in the poppy seeds.

• Pour the mixture into a lined 20cm round tin. I am a big fan of paper tin liners so I use one of these.

• Place the cake on the low rack and bake at 200°C for 35–40 minutes (cooking times depend on the oven's efficiency). To test if the cake is done, press the top gently with a finger. If the sponge springs back, it is cooked.

• If you want to add a lemon drizzle effect, mix the juice of half a lemon with 3–4 teaspoons of xylitol or sugar and pour over the cake while it is still warm. Leave to soak in for 5 minutes before turning out onto a wire rack.

• Serve hot or cold. Store in an airtight container for up to four days.

Did you know? *250 million people worldwide are affected by diabetes. This figure is predicted to rise to 350 million in 2025.*

200g low-fat margarine or butter
200g xylitol or brown sugar
3 eggs
100g polenta flour
200g ground almonds
2 tsp baking powder (or gluten-free baking powder)
Zest of 2–3 lemons
1 tsp lemon extract (optional)
1–2 tbsp poppy seeds

No-added-sugar carrot cupcakes

225g wholemeal
flour
1 tsp baking
powder
2 tsp ground
cinnamon
2 eggs, beaten
150ml light olive oil
175ml apple juice
225g carrots,
peeled and
grated
75g sultanas
50g dates, chopped
30g desiccated
coconut

This sugar-free recipe is really yummy and perfect with a cup of tea. If you really crave additional sweetness, why not make a topping by mixing some Greek yoghurt or low-fat mascarpone with a little icing sugar and vanilla extract?

• Place the flour, baking powder and cinnamon in a bowl and combine well.

• In a jug, mix the eggs with the olive oil. Pour this over the dry ingredients and mix well. Gradually stir in the apple juice.

• Add all the remaining ingredients and combine well.

• Place the silicon muffin cases on a tray and fill to three-quarters.

• Place on the high rack and bake at 190°C for 15–20 minutes. To test if the cupcakes are done, press the top gently with a finger. If the sponge springs back, they are ready. If they are not quite cooked, return to the oven and bake for a further 5 minutes. Machine temperatures vary, so cakes can be a little more unpredictable in the halogen.

• Serve hot or cold.

Seed biscuits

Makes
6–10
(depending on cutter size)

I love these when I'm feeling a little peckish and want a savoury snack. Lovely with cheese but also try with houmous or my personal favourite, mozzarella, sun-dried tomatoes and rocket with a drizzle of balsamic vinegar. Making me hungry just thinking about it!

- Gently melt the coconut oil in a pan.

- In a bowl, rub the butter or margarine into the flour.

- Stir in the melted oil and seeds, adding 180ml of cold water, a little at a time, until you have formed a firm and not too wet dough (you may not need all the water). Season with black pepper.

- Roll out on a floured surface to about 5mm thick and cut out rounds using a biscuit cutter.

- Place on a greased baking tray.

- Place on the high rack and bake in batches at 190°C for 20 minutes or until golden. Do not overcook.

- Store in an airtight container for up to four days.

4 tbsp coconut oil, melted
60g butter or low-fat margarine
400g wholemeal flour
60g mixed seeds
Freshly ground black pepper

Lemon and raspberry cake

225g butter or low-
     fat margarine
200g xylitol
3 medium eggs,
     beaten
180g polenta flour
125g ground
     almonds
Juice and zest of 2
     lemons
1 tsp lemon extract
200g fresh
     raspberries

This recipe uses ground almonds and polenta so is suitable for those on a gluten-free diet. I love this cake served warm with a few fresh raspberries and a dollop of fat-free Greek yoghurt.

• In a bowl, beat the butter with the xylitol until light and fluffy.

• Add the eggs, one at a time. In between adding each egg, add a spoonful of the polenta flour and combine well.

• When all the eggs are mixed in, add the remaining ingredients and combine.

• Line a 20cm springform cake tin with a cake liner and pour the mixture into the tin.

• Place on the low rack and bake at 190°C for 30–40 minutes until golden. To test if the cake is done, insert a skewer or the tip of a sharp knife in the centre of the cake. If it comes out clean (barring any raspberry!), it is cooked; if it comes out wet, it needs a little longer.

• Serve hot or cold.

Carrot seed flapjacks

*I like to add a teaspoon of cinnamon and ground
cardamom in this to add a little bit of warmth, but feel free
to take this out if you don't like the flavours. You can also
add a small handful of sultanas and desiccated coconut if
you wish.*

• In a large pan heat the coconut oil, margarine or
butter, xylitol/sugar, agave syrup, treacle and spices
together, stirring until melted and smooth.

• Remove the pan from the heat and stir in the
carrots, oats and seeds.

• Tip into a greased ovenproof baking tin (I use a
23cm square brownie tin or sandwich tin) and press
down firmly.

• Place on the high rack and bake at 200°C for 15–20
minutes.

• Leave in the tin and cut into slices. Leave to cool
completely before removing the flapjacks from the tin.

50g coconut oil
100g low-fat
   margarine or
   butter
110g xylitol or
   brown sugar
4 tbsp agave syrup
2 tbsp black treacle
1 tsp ground
   cinnamon
1 tsp ground
   cardamom
225g grated carrots
325g oats
3 tbsp pumpkin
   seeds
3 tbsp sunflower
   seeds

Desserts

When following a healthy diet or lifestyle, we all assume that it is the kiss of death to eat anything naughty and nice, but think again! Once you have mastered some of the healthy food swaps in this book, you will be able to adapt some of your favourite recipes. Remember, everything in moderation, but if you satisfy a sweet craving with these healthier choices you are less likely to go raiding the biscuit tin or the children's chocolate stash.

Sugar

You will see that the use of sugar is limited in this book. Instead I opt for natural sweeteners such as xylitol or stevia (see p.11). The good news is these sweetners do not have the negative effects of sugar (or artificial sweeteners), so you can enjoy them guilt-free. Xylitol can be used as a direct replacement for sugar, so for ease of use I have used this in the recipes. If you want to use stevia, then be aware that you need a lot less as it is very sweet. You will need to adjust the quantity to taste or as directed by the manufacturer.

Baked peaches with raspberry and almonds

4 peaches, halved
and stoned
6 tsp agave syrup
2 tsp almond
extract
Small handful of
fresh or frozen
raspberries
Small handful of
flaked almonds
Fat-free Greek
yoghurt, to serve

This is a great recipe for using up store-cupboard ingredients when you want to make a tasty dessert. It tastes nicer with fresh peaches but you can use tinned if out of season.

• Place the peaches in your ovenproof dish, flat side up.

• In a small bowl, mix the agave syrup with the almond extract and spoon into the centre of the peaches. Add a few raspberries in the centre (if frozen they do not have to be defrosted).

• Sprinkle with the flaked almonds.

• Place on the low rack and bake at 180°C for 20–25 minutes.

• Serve with a dollop of fat-free Greek yoghurt.

Healthy tip! *This recipe uses agave syrup so you get the sweetness while keeping your blood-sugar levels balanced.*

Chocolate and ginger cheesecake

It is really nice to have the occasional treat, especially if you are watching your weight. This recipe feels like a very rich treat but is low in fat and sugar. I always opt for xylitol – stevia is good but it can be a bit hit and miss to get the right sweetness – too much and it can leave a chemical after-taste. Always use Greek yoghurt as it keeps its shape during cooking. I use Total, but some supermarkets are doing their own versions, which can be just as good.

• Melt the margarine in a saucepan. Remove from the heat, add the biscuits and combine well. Tip into a greased 20–22cm springform cake tin and press down firmly with the back of a spoon. Refrigerate while you complete the next phase.

• In a bowl, combine the egg yolks with the xylitol and beat until light and fluffy. Stir in the cream cheese and yoghurt.

• Melt the chocolate. You can do this in a bain-marie (place a bowl over a saucepan of boiling water – but don't let the water touch the base of the bowl) or in a microwave (be careful not to overcook – about 30 seconds is enough). Once melted, combine with the creamed mixture.

• Whisk the egg whites until they form stiff peaks. Fold into the mixture, then pour over the biscuit base. Cover with foil.

• Place on the low rack and bake at 150°C for 50 minutes. Leave to cool completely in the tin before refrigerating.

• Sprinkle a little grated dark chocolate on the top before serving with some fresh raspberries and a dollop of Greek yoghurt.

150g low-fat
    margarine
175g Nairns ginger
    oat biscuits,
    crushed
2 medium eggs,
    separated
75g xylitol
300g low-fat cream
    cheese
200g fat-free Greek
    yoghurt
100g dark
    chocolate (at
    least 70%
    cocoa), plus
    extra to garnish
Fresh raspberries
    and fat-free
    Greek yoghurt,
    to serve

Healthy tip! *Nairns biscuits are suitable for those following a gluten-free diet.*

Strawberry tarts

250g strawberries
3 tbsp fat-free
Greek yoghurt
3 tbsp low-fat
cream cheese
3–4 sheets of filo
pastry
2 tbsp coconut oil,
melted
4 tbsp raspberry
coulis

As these tarts are made with filo pastry they are easier on the waistline than shortcrust pastry. I brush the pastry with coconut oil as it is a healthy option, but you can use butter if you prefer. Use silicon cupcake moulds, ramekins, individual deep cake moulds or individual tart dishes. I prefer to use ramekins or deep moulds as I like to create high pastry sides for extra crunch.

• Place half the strawberries in a food processor. Add the yoghurt and cream cheese and beat well. Transfer to a bowl and chill for at least 1 hour.

• Line six very well-greased ramekins with the filo pastry, brushing with coconut oil as you go. Make sure the pastry sheets overlap to create a sealed base. Line with baking parchment and fill with baking beans. If you don't have baking beans, use dried pulses or uncooked rice instead.

• Place on the low rack and blind bake at 210°C for 5 minutes. Blind baking gives a head start on the cooking as pastry doesn't always cook that well in the halogen oven.

• Remove the baking beans and baking parchment, and cook for a further 5–8 minutes until the pastry is crisp and golden.

• Leave the pastry cases to cool, then remove them very carefully from the ramekins as they are delicate.

• When ready to serve, remove the yoghurt mixture from the fridge. Carefully stir in half of the raspberry coulis – don't over-mix, as you want a ripple effect.

• Place a few sliced strawberries in the bottom of the pastry cases and drizzle with a little of the remaining coulis.

• Spoon the yoghurt mixture into the pastry cases.

• Top with a few more strawberries and a dribble of coulis. Serve immediately.

Roasted fruit compote

This delicious compote can be served to accompany porridge for breakfast or as a satisfying dessert. Add a dollop of fat-free Greek yoghurt for extra creaminess. Want a quick and easy crumble? Why not crumble some delicious sweet oat biscuits over the top or add a handful of your favourite muesli.

• Place the fresh and dried fruit, apart from the blueberries, in an ovenproof dish. Add the orange juice and zest and orange wedges. Combine well.

• Place on the low rack and cook at 180°C for 15 minutes.

• Add the blueberries and syrup and combine again. Return to the oven and cook for a further 10 minutes.

• Serve hot or cold.

Did you know? *Blueberries are a great source of the flavonoid anthocyanin – a powerful antioxidant that has been shown to have anti-inflammatory properties.*

---

2 cooking apples, skins on, sliced into wedges

1 pear, skin on, sliced into wedges

1–2 nectarines or peaches, stoned and quartered

Small handful of dried apricots or figs

Juice and zest of 1 orange

1 orange, peeled and cut into wedges

150g blueberries

2–3 tbsp agave syrup

Rhubarb crumble

650g rhubarb,
chopped to
2–3cm length
50g xylitol or brown
sugar (to taste)
200g wholemeal
flour
30g ground
almonds
60g oats
100g low-fat spread
25g brown sugar
Fat-free Greek
yoghurt, to serve

I love rhubarb. There's nothing nicer than picking it fresh from the garden and making this delicious dessert. Serve with fat-free Greek yoghurt.

• Place the rhubarb in a saucepan and add the xylitol/sugar, along with 50–100ml of water. Cook gently for 5–8 minutes to soften the fruit. Pour into an ovenproof dish.

• In a bowl, combine the flour, ground almonds and oats. Rub in the low-fat spread to form a texture similar to breadcrumbs. Add the sugar and combine well.

• Pour over the fruit base, making sure it is spread evenly.

• Place on the low rack and cook at 190°C for 20 minutes.

• Serve with a dollop of yoghurt.

Did you know? *If you are overweight you are over one hundred times more likely to suffer from diabetes.*

Baked cinnamon apples

A traditional autumnal treat.

• Preheat the halogen oven to 220°C or use the preheat setting.

• Wash and core the apples but do not peel them. In a small bowl, mix the agave syrup or honey with 10ml of boiling water and the cinnamon. Stir until dissolved.

• Place the apples on a baking tray or ovenproof dish and add 2 tablespoons of water to the dish. Brush the apples with the honey mixture.

• Stuff the cores of the apples with sultanas and finish with a sprinkling of brown sugar.

• Place on the low rack and bake for 20–30 minutes until soft.

• Serve with low-fat crème fraîche or natural yoghurt.

4 Bramley apples
2 tsp agave syrup
or runny honey
2–3 tsp ground
cinnamon
30g sultanas
1 tsp brown sugar
Low-fat crème
fraîche or natural
yoghurt, to serve

Did you know? *Apples are a good source of quercetin, which can help prevent thickening of the arteries.*

150g blueberries
300ml fat-free
  Greek yoghurt
1 tsp vanilla paste
4 egg yolks
1 tbsp cornflour
4 tbsp brown sugar

Vanilla and blueberry brûlée

You will be surprised how easy these are to make. Ideal for dinner parties but also as a guilt-free pleasure.

• Divide the blueberries between four ramekins.

• In a bowl, combine the yoghurt, vanilla paste, egg yolks and cornflour together. I use a hand blender for this. Pour into the ramekins.

• Boil the kettle. Place the ramekins in the base of the halogen oven and carefully pour boiling water around the ramekins until about halfway up the sides.

• Set the temperature to 180°C and bake for 30 minutes. Lift them out and leave to cool. Refrigerate for 30 minutes before serving.

• When ready to serve, sprinkle with the sugar. Place on the high rack, making sure the dishes don't touch the element. Set the temperature to high and caramelise the tops until they turn golden. Keep an eye on the brûlées, as they can burn!

• Serve immediately.

Did you know? *Blueberries are a great source of the flavonoid anthocyanin – a powerful antioxidant that can help prevent free-radical damage.*

Fruit kebabs

Healthy desserts can be absolutely delicious! Okay, the inclusion of the dark chocolate is an extra incentive to give it a go!

• Thread the fruit pieces onto skewers (if using wooden ones, make sure you pre-soak them).

• Brush with a little Sweet Freedom syrup.

• Place directly on the high rack and grill at 230°C for a few minutes on each side, turning occasionally.

• Meanwhile, place the remaining ingredients in a pan over a medium heat. Gently melt and combine to form a sauce, stirring all the time to prevent burning.

• Serve the kebabs with the chocolate dipping sauce.

Variety of fruit (banana, pineapple, strawberry, kiwi, apple, peach, nectarine, etc), chopped

2 tbsp Sweet Freedom syrup, plus extra for brushing

75g dark chocolate (at least 70% cocoa)

3 tbsp skimmed milk

1 tsp cocoa powder

Did you know? *Dark chocolate doesn't spike your blood-sugar levels like dairy chocolate, but it has to have at least 70 per cent cocoa content. Eating one or two chunks of good-quality dark chocolate a day has been shown to have health benefits due to the high antioxidant content.*

Summer berries healthy brûlée

200g fresh or
frozen berries (I
use frozen
summer berries)
350–400g fat-free
Greek yoghurt
3 tbsp low-fat
crème fraîche
1 tsp vanilla paste
3–4 tbsp brown
sugar or Sweet
Freedom syrup
(see box)

*This is a really yummy dessert that takes minutes to
prepare. It looks and tastes far more impressive than it
really is and the good news is it is actually quite healthy!
You can use whatever fresh fruit you like – raspberries,
strawberries or a combination of berries is lovely.*

• If you are using frozen berries, divide them into
serving glasses to defrost. If you want to speed up the
process, place them in an ovenproof dish and pop
them on the low rack and heat at 200°C for 2 minutes.

• Meanwhile, mix the yoghurt and crème fraîche
together in a bowl, then add the vanilla paste and stir
well.

• If you are using fresh berries, divide them into
serving glasses.

• Spoon over the yoghurt mixture.

• For those of you who don't worry about calories,
sprinkle enough brown sugar on top of the yoghurt to
form a generous layer.

• Place on the high rack at 235°C and caramelise to
form a golden layer. Do not leave the brûlées
unattended as they can burn quite quickly.

• You can serve them immediately, but they are best
served chilled.

NB: Xylitol does not have the same caramelising
properties as sugar, so you can't use it for the topping.

---

*Healthy swap! For an extra-healthy topping, just add a
drizzle of Sweet Freedom syrup instead of the brown sugar
(no need to caramelise).*

Baked honey and ginger pears

2–4 pears, peeled, halved and cored
Runny honey
4–8 ginger biscuits, crumbled
1 tsp mixed spice
Vanilla ice cream, to serve

If you opt for gluten-free ginger biscuits, this recipe is suitable for those on a gluten-free diet.

• Place the pears on a browning tray flat side up. Drizzle over a small amount of honey – try to keep it in the centre of the pears so it does not run onto the tray.

• Place on the high rack and bake at 220°C for 10–15 minutes.

• Meanwhile, crush the ginger biscuits. Place them in a plastic food bag and bash with a rolling pin.

• Remove the pears from the oven and drizzle with more honey and a sprinkle of mixed spice. Cover with the crumbled ginger biscuits.

• Return to the oven and cook for a further 5–10 minutes, or until soft.

• Serve with a generous dollop of vanilla ice cream.

Serves
4

2 cooking apples,
  peeled and
  chopped
1 tbsp xylitol or
  brown sugar
2–3 sheets of filo
  pastry
1 tbsp coconut oil,
  melted
2 tbsp mincemeat
Greek yoghurt, to
  serve

Apple and mincemeat tarts

As these tarts are made with filo pastry they are easier on the waistline than shortcrust pastry. I brush the pastry with coconut oil as it is a healthy option, but you can use butter if you prefer. Use silicon cupcake moulds, ramekins, individual deep cake moulds or individual tart dishes. I prefer to use ramekins or deep moulds as I like to create high pastry sides for extra crunch.

• Place the apples, xylitol/sugar and 1 tablespoon of water in a saucepan and cook gently on a low/medium heat until the apple starts to soften but still hold its shape.

• Meanwhile, line four greased ramekins with the filo pastry, brushing with coconut oil as you go. Make sure the pastry sheets overlap to create a sealed base. Line with baking parchment and fill with baking beans. If you don't have baking beans, use dried pulses or uncooked rice instead.

• Place on the low rack and blind bake at 210°C for 5 minutes. Blind baking gives a head start on the cooking as pastry doesn't always cook that well in the halogen oven.

• Remove the baking beans and baking parchment and add a little mincemeat to each ramekin, followed by the cooked apple.

• Return to the oven and cook for a further 5–10 minutes until the pastry is crisp and golden.

• Serve with a dollop of Greek yoghurt.

Baked banana apples with ricotta cream

Serve the stuffed apples with this delicious ricotta cream for extra indulgence.

• Wash and core the apples but do not peel them. Place them on a greased or lined baking tray.

• In a bowl, mix the bananas, nutmeg, cinnamon, lemon juice and sugar together. Fill the cores of the apples with the banana mixture.

• Place the apples on the high rack and cook at 190°C for 30–40 minutes until they are tender.

• Meanwhile, mix the ricotta and yoghurt with the vanilla, honey and cinnamon.

• Remove the apples from the oven and place on warmed plates, with a generous dollop of the ricotta cream.

Did you know? Bananas are rich in potassium and vitamins C and B6.

4 cooking apples
2–3 soft bananas, mashed
$1/4$ tsp nutmeg
1 tsp cinnamon
15ml lemon juice
2 tbsp brown sugar
110g ricotta cheese
50ml Greek yoghurt
$1/2$ tsp vanilla extract
1 tbsp runny honey
$1/2$ tsp cinnamon

4–6

Gooseberry and elderflower healthy brûlée

250g gooseberries
4 tbsp elderflower
cordial
350–400g fat-free
Greek yoghurt
3 tbsp low-fat
crème fraîche
1 tsp vanilla paste
3–4 tbsp brown
sugar or Sweet
Freedom syrup
(see below)

This is a really yummy dessert that takes minutes to prepare. It looks and tastes far more impressive than it really is and the good news is it is actually quite healthy! I love gooseberries and wish their season was longer, but I do try to freeze as many as I can so they last longer.

• Place the gooseberries in a saucepan and add the cordial. Heat very gently until the gooseberries start to pop and soften. Remove from the heat and allow to cool. Some people find gooseberries need a little sugar; personally, I like them without, but feel free to taste and add a little sugar or xylitol to taste.

• Mix the yoghurt and crème fraîche together in a bowl, then add the vanilla paste and stir well.

• Place the cooled gooseberries in individual dishes or in one larger serving dish. Spoon over the yoghurt mixture.

• For those of you who don't worry about calories, sprinkle enough brown sugar on top of the yoghurt to form a generous layer.

• Place on the high rack at 235°C and caramelise to form a golden layer. Do not leave the brûlées unattended as they can burn quite quickly.

• You can serve them immediately but they are best served chilled.

NB: Xylitol does not have the same caramelising properties as sugar, so you can't use it for the topping.

Healthy swap! For an extra-healthy topping, just add a drizzle of Sweet Freedom syrup instead of the brown sugar (no need to caramelise).

Warm chocolate brownies

I am a chocolate addict, so these are a firm favourite in our house. We love these brownies warm with a dollop of fat-free Greek yoghurt or low-fat crème fraîche. They are just as good cold. Store them in an airtight container for up to four days.

- Put the oil, xylitol and eggs in a bowl and whisk until light and fluffy.

- In a cup, mix the coffee and cocoa powder with 3 tablespoons of hot water.

- Put the yoghurt and vanilla extract in a bowl and pour in the coffee mixture. Add all this to the egg mixture, then sift in the flour.

- Melt the dark chocolate in the microwave (gently for 30 seconds) or in a bain-marie, and stir into the batter.

- Pour the batter into a lined and greased 16cm square baking or brownie tray.

- Place on the low rack and bake at 190°C for 20–25 minutes. You want the brownie to be a little bit gooey in the middle, so don't overcook it as it can go quite dry.

NB: If you are a chocolate addict, you could add some chocolate chips to the mixture. For a more chewy texture, add a small handful of chopped dates.

3 tbsp coconut oil
150g xylitol
2 eggs
$1/2$ tsp good-quality instant coffee granules
1 heaped tbsp cocoa powder
90g fat-free Greek yoghurt
1 tsp vanilla extract
100g self-raising flour
100g dark chocolate (at least 70% cocoa)

Index